米麵簡餐

與小菜、甜點

CHINESE
RICE AND NOODLES

WITH · APPETIZERS · SOUPS · AND · SWEETS

作者：黃淑惠
烹飪製作：李木村

企劃編輯
賴燕貞、郭心怡

文稿協助
柯文敏、馬優雅
陳素貞

翻譯
何久恩、張方馨
陳美君、翁盛靈

攝影
迷彩廣告攝影 廖家威

美術編輯
張方馨、黃雯雯

電腦排版
洪明慧

分色製版
中華彩色印刷股份有限公司

印刷
中華彩色印刷股份有限公司

味全出版社
版權所有
2005年9月初版 1-0-5
2008年9月2版 2-0-92

Author
Su-Huei Huang

Dish Presentation
Mu-Tsun Lee

Managing Editors
Yen-Jen Lai
Margaret Kuo

Editorial Staff
Leila Ko
Gloria Martinez

Translation
John Holt
Fandra Chang
Meghan Chen
Kelley Weng

Photography
Camo Studio
Liao Chia Wei

Design
Fandra Chang
Wen Wen Huang

Wei-Chuan Publishing
1455 Monterey Pass Rd.,
Suite 110,
Monterey Park, CA 91754,
U.S.A.

Tel: 323-261-3880
Fax: 323-261-3299
wc@weichuancookbook.com
www.weichuancookbook.com

First Printing
September 2005

Secend Printing
September 2008

ISBN 13: 978-0-941676-86-1
ISBN 10: 0-941676-86-2
(Chinese/English)

Printed in Taiwan

目錄 TABLE of CONTENTS

序 *Introduction*

由於時代變遷與生活步調的加速，講求效率，已鮮少花長時間來準備傳統的數道主菜配一湯的組合。為了讓讀者在忙碌的生活中能在家享受口味道地的中國菜，本書在製作之初即以調理方式簡易、敘述條理化、材料簡便易取得為準則，編輯內容除收集已絕版的『中國簡餐』及多增加大眾喜愛的菜色外，再搭配小菜及甜點，並以簡餐的方式呈現給讀者，讓讀者在短時間內即能料理出簡便美味的一餐。

本書包涵46道米食、37道麵食，並附加26道小菜、5道湯及30道甜點，讀者可任取一道米食或麵食成簡易的一餐，也可在簡餐上搭配小菜、湯或甜點成豐富的套餐。無論是家常便飯或是朋友歡聚時光，期許這本書能成為讀者最實用的料理參考書籍之一。

本書從企劃、編輯、試菜、設計至出版皆在美國完成，在編輯過程中承蒙賴燕貞及郭心怡協助搜集及企劃編輯，柯文敏協助試做及文稿整理，何久恩翻譯，張方馨及黃雯雯的設計，讓本書在保留傳統味全食譜的優點之際同時展現新的風格。最後感謝多年合作夥伴李木村老師鼎力協助，利用他在日本的『魚翅海鮮中國菜館』做最後一次試菜及完成所有菜餚的製作，並榮幸使用餐廳內的精緻瓷器裝盤，順利完成攝影作業。

Chinese Rice and Noodles was written in the recognition that the pace of everyday life has increased dramatically and that we seldom have the luxury of time to prepare traditional multi-course meals. This cookbook addresses both the readers' fast-paced lifestyles and the desire for delicious meals that can be prepared at home by offering authentic Chinese cuisine in simplified steps, streamlined procedures, and with readily available ingredients. Simplified recipes from the highly acclaimed and now out-of-print *Chinese One Dish Meals*, additional popular dishes, appetizers and desserts comprise this book. Presented in one-dish format, these easy recipes enable readers to create delicious meals with little effort.

This cookbook contains 46 rice dishes, 37 noodle dishes, 26 side dishes, 5 soups, and 30 desserts. Readers may choose a rice or noodle dish for a quick meal or embellish the simple meal with a soup, a side dish, and dessert for a complete meal. For daily meals or for social gatherings, the reader will find this cookbook to be one of the most practical and often used culinary references in their collection of cookbooks.

From planning, editing, recipe testing, designing, and publishing, this cookbook was prepared entirely in the United States. Thanks to the following collaborators, this cookbook maintains Wei-Chuan Cookbook's tradition of excellence while simultaneously showcasing the latest culinary favorites. The diligent research and planning skills of Yen-Jen Lai and Margaret Kuo underpinned the editing process. Leila Ko assisted in recipe testing and manuscript preparation while John Holt provided translation. The cookbook owes its design to Fandra Chang and Wen Wen Huang. Finally, my gratitude goes to my long-time collaborator Master Chef Mu-Tsun Lee for his stalwart support and expert guidance. The final testing of all the recipes was conducted at his "Lee's Garden Seafood Chinese Restaurant" in Japan, and the dishes were photographed on the restaurant's exquisite China serving-ware collection.

Sa Huei Huang

黃淑惠女士

於1963年創立台北味全家政班，1972年出版第一本食譜『中國菜』，此書暢銷全球，再版67次，銷售量突破百萬本，至今仍深受好評。1979年成立美國味全出版社，並陸續出版多本雙語食譜，翻譯成多種語言，除將中華美食文化推向世界舞台外，並將味全食譜由中國菜領域拓展至異國風味。

秉持每道菜親自試作、敘述簡潔明瞭及嚴格審核食譜內容的一貫理念，黃女士個人著作包括『中國菜』、『點心專輯』、『實用中國菜』、『拼盤與盤飾』、『米麵簡餐』等等。親任總編輯並聘請專家協力製作的食譜包括：『速簡中國菜』、『實用家庭菜』、『泰國菜』、『墨西哥菜』、『韓國菜』、『越南菜』及『南洋菜』等。

李木村先生

台灣省台北縣人，目前旅居日本，在日本神戶市經營『魚翅海鮮中國菜館』，2004年被日本電視台、婦人畫報、家庭畫報等有名雜誌譽選為『日本神戶最好的中國菜館』。目前兼任西宮甲子園短期大學中國菜點講師。

專研美食三十餘年，致力推廣中華美食文化，曾任日本調理師學校中國料理主任教授、美國 New Meiji 連鎖快餐公司指導、台灣中華電視台中國菜示範及味全烹飪學校教師。著有『速簡中國菜』，並協力製作『中國菜』、『實用中國菜』、『拼盤與盤飾』等十餘本味全食譜。

Su-Huei Huang In 1963, Ms. Huang established the Wei-Chuan Cooking School in Taipei. She published her first cookbook, *Chinese Cuisine*, in 1972. *Chinese Cuisine* was widely sold all over the world and enjoyed reprinting 67 times; to date, it has sold over one million copies, and it remains highly acclaimed. Wei-Chuan Publishing was established in the United States in 1979. Wei-Chuan Publishing subsequently produced numerous bilingual cookbooks, many of which were translated into multiple languages so that in addition to showcasing the beauty of Chinese cuisine on the world stage, Wei-Chuan cookbooks could also provide a vehicle to broaden culinary appreciation of exotic flavors in various nations.

Ms. Huang personally experimented with each recipe, clarified explanations, and simplified procedures for all of her cookbooks. She also vigorously scrutinized the thematic development and organization of all of her works. Ms. Huang authored *Chinese Cuisine, Chinese Snacks, Chinese Cooking for Beginners, Chinese Appetizers and Garnishes, Chinese Rice and Noodles,* and more. Additionally, as editor-in-chief, Ms. Huang called on experts to collaborate on such titles as *Chinese Cooking Made Easy, Chinese Favorite Home Dishes, Thai Cooking Made Easy, Mexican Cooking Made Easy, Korean Cuisine, Vietnamese Cuisine* and *Singaporean Malaysian & Indonesian Cuisine.*

Mu-Tsun Lee A native son of Taipei, Taiwan, Mr. Lee now resides in Japan. He owns the "Lee's Garden Seafood Chinese Restaurant", recently honored as the best Chinese restaurant in Kobe, Japan, by the MBS television station, Fujingaho and Katei Gaho magazines. Presently, Mr. Lee also teaches Chinese cooking to aspiring chefs at Koshien Junior College in Nishinomiya, Japan.

Mr. Lee has been studying and teaching culinary arts for over thirty years; he steadfastly advocates broad promotion of the Chinese culinary culture. He has held the position of Chief Professor of Chinese cooking at a cooking school in Japan and is the chief consultant of New Meiji franchised restaurants in the United States. While in Taiwan, he demonstrated his skills on the Chinese Television System, "Chinese Cooking Show", and taught cooking classes at the Wei-Chuan Cooking School. He authored *Chinese Cooking Made Easy* and collaborated on *Chinese Cuisine, Chinese Cooking for Beginners, Chinese Appetizers and Garnishes,* and over ten other Wei-Chuan cookbooks.

米麵東西南北

Rice and Noodles East · West · North & South

中國地大遼闊，其各地的農作物、飲食文化等也隨地理位置及氣候的不同而變化繁多，一般來說南方種稻，以米食為主，北方地區盛產小麥，則以麵食為主。本書以簡餐為主，故僅挑選適於當簡餐且受歡迎的傳統菜餚，再加上一些近代新風味的美食及中國各地的粥、粉、飯、麵與台灣小吃等精華，各個不同區域的菜餚都具其特色，以下略做簡單介紹：

The vastness of China encompasses greatly varied climates and geography yielding different produce, grains, and formulations of a culinary culture. Generally, southern China grows rice as a staple, while wheat flourishes in the north. Since this cookbook is about easy meals, all recipes have been selected based on suitability for one dish meals and on popularity of traditional favorites. The addition of newly embraced dishes and numerous congee, rice and noodle meals from different regions in addition to Taiwanese snacks, make this an exciting collection of treasured classics and new favorites. The following is a brief introduction to the unique regional cuisines:

四川菜 以多用辣椒、花椒等辛辣調味為出名，如乾燒、魚香、麻辣、椒麻等各種味型，是喜食辣味者的最愛！著名的有宮保雞丁、麻婆豆腐等。湖南菜也是以辛辣為特色，常與川菜並稱，但不如川味麻辣。

Szechwan Cuisine is legendary for its spiciness based in chilies, peppercorns, and other spicy sauces. Flavors such as *spicy ketchup sauce, spicy garlic sauce, numbing chili sauce, Szechwan pepper and sesame sauce* are sure to please chili lovers. Well-known signature dishes include "Kung Pao Chicken" and "Ma-Po Tofu". Hunan cuisine is also appreciated for its spicy character just as Szechwan cuisine, although Hunan spiciness is not as intense as its Szechwan counterpart.

廣東菜 匯集中西各地飲食精華，調味品五花八門，例如豉汁、蠔油、海鮮醬、沙茶醬等，從家常菜到宴客菜烹調花樣多且富變化。著名的飲茶也是廣東菜。

Cantonese Cuisine a repository of culinary creativity from eastern and western regions, offers innumerable sauces such as *black bean sauce, oyster sauce, hoisin sauce,* and *Sa-Tsa BBQ paste.* From home cooking to restaurant banquets, Cantonese cuisine manifests itself in dynamic creations and new varieties. The celebrated dim sum is also part of Cantonese cuisine.

新疆 Xinjiang
甘肅 Gansu
青海 Qinghai
西藏 Tibet
四 SZECH
雲南 Yunnan

北方菜 融合了中國北方各地精華，以肉類及麵食為主，較少海鮮。除有名的羊肉料理外，以薄餅搭配北平烤鴨或木肉等吃法亦為北方菜的特色之一。

Beijing Cuisine blends the best flavors in the northern region featuring meats and flour-based staples, with less emphasis on seafood. Besides the renowned lamb dishes, this cuisine's exceptional offerings include lotus crepes that accompany "Peking Duck" and "Mu-Shu Pork".

江浙菜 集上海、蘇州、杭州等地方菜，有些菜餚以色深口味偏甜為特色，中國菜內廣泛使用的烹調技巧『紅燒』即源自此處。著名的有紅燒獅子頭、上海菜飯等。

Shanghai Cuisine is an amalgamation of Shanghai, Soochow, and Hangchow cuisines. The food's distinctive characteristics are darker coloring and a penchant for sweetness. The frequently employed cooking technique of *braising in soy sauce* originated in this region. Prominent dishes include "Lion's Head on Rice" and "Shanghai Rice with Greens".

台灣菜 以調味清淡，保留原味的海產及環繞市集的小吃為特色。切阿麵、肉羹、蚵仔麵線等即為著名的台灣小吃，充分表現出台灣特殊的飲食文化。

Taiwanese Cuisine tends to have light seasoning, retaining the original flavors of the surrounding sea's bounty as well as the side and snack dishes of the street vendors. Famous dishes include "Chi-Ah Noodle Soup", "Pork and Mushroom Noodle Chowder", "Oyster Soup with Thin Noodles", fully expressing the individuality of Taiwanese cuisine.

中華料理區域圖 Map of Chinese Regional Cuisines

米飯是中國人不可缺少的主食之一，米的種類很多，白米是最廣為食用的。近年來健康飲食蔚為風尚，糙米、五穀米、雜糧也逐漸的被大眾喜愛，喜歡白米飯卻又考量健康因素的人，可將白米與糙米或五穀雜糧混合煮成飯；此外，有些人在米飯或粥之內添加蕃薯、黃豆或其他蔬菜加以變化。

米的種類

1. 白米 稻穀去除穀殼及米糠的米，米粒半透明，一般依其外觀分長型(在來米)及圓型(蓬萊米)。長型米的特性是煮熟的米飯較無黏性且乾鬆，呈顆粒狀，在中國內陸、東南亞一帶、中東或西方國家等頗為盛行；圓型米則是煮熟後的米飯較有黏性且較軟，在日本、韓國、台灣一帶多食用這種米。

2. 糙米 稻穀去除穀殼後仍帶有米糠的米粒即為糙米。糙米飯較白米飯含更多的纖維與維生素，可促進新陳代謝、幫助腸胃消化蠕動。煮熟的飯雖然不像白米飯那麼的香軟，但多了一番嚼勁，越嚼越香甜且易有飽足感。

3. 糯米 一般為白色不透明的米粒，常用來做鹹甜點。糯米又分長型及圓型。長型糯米煮後較有嚼勁，多用來煮油飯，飯糰等鹹點，長糯米除白糯米外還有黑糯米俗稱紫米，營養價值高，常用於養生食譜。圓型糯米煮熟後較有黏性，常用來做中式甜點如八寶粥、甜粽等。

4. 五穀米 包括蕎麥、燕麥、小米、黑糯米、薏仁、糙米、胚芽米等等多種雜糧所組成的穀類，含有豐富的纖維素與維他命B群，五穀米飯營養價值高。市場售有已配好的五穀米。

1　　2　　3

Rice is one of the most indispensable staple foods for the Chinese. It is valued for its versatility, as well as for its nutritional benefits; rich in complex carbohydrates, protein, minerals, fiber and vitamins. There are various types of rice, with white rice being the most popular. Brown rice, multigrain rice and other grains have gained tremendous popularity due to recent health conscious trends. For those who desire the nutritional values of brown rice but prefer the taste of white rice, brown or multigrain rice may be mixed with white rice during cooking. Additionally, yams, soybeans or other vegetables may also be added to rice and congee to create more variety and alternative healthy choices.

Types of Rice

1. White rice The rice grain is removed from its kernel and bran, creating fully milled or "polished" white rice which is semi-translucent. Generally classified according to its shape: long grain or short grain rice. When cooked, the long grain rice remains separate and maintains its shape, its characteristics tend to be dry, fluffy, less sticky than the short grain rice. Long grain rice is popular in Mainland China, Southeast Asia, Middle East and Western countries, while short grain rice is more popular in Japan, Korea and Taiwan.

2. Brown rice The rice is removed from its kernel but retains its bran, thus containing more fiber and vitamins than white rice. Brown rice helps increase metabolism and stimulates the digestive system. Though it lacks the fragrance and softness of white rice, it is preferred for its health benefits, nutty flavor and chewy texture, and it is satisfying and very filling.

3. Glutinous rice Also known as sticky or sweet rice, glutinous rice is opaque, and is often used in savory snacks and sweet desserts. There are two types of glutinous rice: long grain and short grain. When cooked, long grain glutinous rice is chewier and is often used in savory snacks such as "Taiwanese Sticky Rice" (p.65). Long grain glutinous rice comes in white and black varieties, also called "purple rice". *Purple rice* is highly nutritious and is often used in Chinese herbal cooking. The short grain glutinous rice becomes sticky when cooked, and is often used to make sweet Chinese desserts.

4. Multigrain rice Multigrain rice is a combination of a wide variety of grains, such as buckwheat, oat meal, millet, black glutinous rice, barley, brown rice, and rice germ, etc. Multigrain is nutritious, rich in vitamin B complex and fiber, and therefore is considered a prime choice and main staple for many people. Prepackaged multigrain rice is readily available in most supermarkets.

4

About Rice

煮飯所需水量

煮飯時可參考米袋包裝說明及電鍋使用說明來煮。一般煮飯原則是：白米與水的比例為1：1；糯米與水的比例為1:2/3；煮糙米與五穀米的水量比煮白米時多。因新舊米所用的水量不同，需留意水的使用量，讀者可依買來的米第一次煮出的結果自行調整水量。只要水量控制得宜即可煮出好吃的米飯。

米、飯的吃法與變化

米飯有很多種食用方式，以下是最常見的：

1. **燴飯** 將煮好帶有濃稠湯汁的菜餚淋在飯上即成香濃可口的燴飯。
2. **炒飯** 將飯與各種配料如火腿、肉絲、蛋、蔬菜等在油鍋內拌炒。
3. **粥** 將生米或飯加多量水煮成無調味的清粥，或加配料一起煮成鹹或甜粥。
4. **蒸菜飯** 將米與蔬菜或肉等配料一起入電鍋裡蒸熟。

Cooking Rice

Depending on the type of rice being used, follow instructions on the rice package and rice cooker. The general rule is use 1 part of white rice with 1 part of water; 1 part of glutinous rice with 2/3 parts of water. More water is needed to cook multigrain rice and brown rice. New rice and aged rice also require different amounts of water. Carefully notice the amount of water used based on the results of the first preparation, then adjust accordingly. To achieve a pot of delicious rice, it is vital that the proper amount of water and correct timing is used.

Variations on Rice Recipes

There are many ways to cook and enjoy rice, below are some of the most common:

1. **Sauce over Rice** A thick and saucy liquid is poured over cooked rice to make a rich and smooth rice dish.
2. **Fried Rice** Stir-fry cooked rice with ingredients such as ham, sliced meats, eggs, and vegetables.
3. **Congee** Cooked or uncooked rice is boiled in a large amount of water until liquid thickens and rice becomes soft; making a plain congee. Additional ingredients are added to make savory or sweet congee.
4. **Steamed Rice Casserole** Rice, vegetables and/or meats are cooked together in a rice cooker.

有關炒飯

基本上先爆香辛香料再加些配料、飯及調味料於鍋內一起翻炒，炒飯所需要的各種材料說明如下：

辛香料 炒飯時常用蒜、蔥白或洋蔥，可任選一兩樣在油鍋內炒出香味。至於蔥綠或香菜類可切碎留在起鍋前撒上，可增香味及色彩。

配料 蛋是炒飯的最佳伙伴，可增加香味還可吸收多餘的水份，冰箱內現成的肉絲、絞肉、香腸、火腿，蝦仁，青豆仁、青椒、番茄、玉米或紅蘿蔔等，都可隨意選一種或數種加入搭配。

飯 用冷飯最適合，冰過的飯通常會結成塊，入鍋前可先將飯壓鬆，這樣在鍋內炒拌時就容易多了。飯放入鍋內時應有適量的油以避免黏鍋。炒飯時需用大火快炒，故一次炒的份量不宜太多。

調味料 最常使用的是鹽、醬油及胡椒等。炒飯因加入不同調味料，顏色不同味道也不一樣，炒飯加入醬油會呈褐色，加入咖哩粉呈黃色，若用番茄醬則呈紅色。

有關粥

粥又稱稀飯，因各地飲食習慣不同，煮粥的濃稠度不一，吃粥的方式也不太相同。有些地方吃清粥配小菜，有些地方則將米與肉類、蔬菜或乾貨等一起煮成鹹或甜粥。廣東粥傳統用長型米，熬煮1 1/2小時以上至粥汁濃稠幾乎不見米粒；台式粥通常使用圓型米，煮的時間較短僅煮至米粒熟軟，剛煮好的粥尚有很多湯汁，靜置一段時間後米粒會繼續吸收湯汁而膨漲變軟。

鹹粥在煮好後通常會撒上芹菜末、蔥末、生薑絲或香菜末來提味。中式芹菜末的提味效果比西式芹菜末好，食譜內提香用的芹菜末皆使用中式芹菜。

About Fried Rice

The general rule in stir-frying is to stir-fry the herbs and spices until fragrant, then add cooked rice, various ingredients and seasonings. It is easy to make up your own favorite recipes, but be sure to follow some of the basic tips included. Below are some of the most commonly used ingredients:

Herbs and Spices Chopped garlic, onions and the white sections of green onions are the most common aromatics used in fried rice; choose one or two and stir-fry in hot oil until fragrant. To add additional aromas and colors, sprinkle minced cilantro or green sections of green onions on the fried rice just prior to removal from wok.

Complements Scrambled eggs are the most favored companions to fried rice; they add aroma and absorb excess liquid from the fried rice. Any combination of available ingredients in the refrigerator, such as sliced, shredded or ground meats, sausage, ham, shelled shrimp, green peas, green bell peppers, tomatoes, corn, and carrots are great complements to the fried rice.

Rice Cold or refrigerated rice is the best, (this is when leftover rice is most useful); using warm or freshly cooked rice may cause the fried rice to turn soggy. Refrigerated rice tends to clump together, pressing and separating the rice prior to stir-frying makes the cooking process easier. Sufficient oil is necessary to prevent rice from sticking to the wok. It is essential to stir-fry rice quickly, in high heat; it is best not to add too much rice at once.

Seasonings The most common seasonings used are salt, soy sauce and pepper. Seasonings not only contribute to the flavor of the dish, but also to its color. Soy sauce turns the fried rice brown; curry powder yellow; and tomato sauce or ketchup turns the fried rice red.

About Congee

Congee is also known as "porridge". Depending on the cultural and culinary preferences, congee is cooked in different consistencies and enjoyed differently throughout various regions of China. Some regions prefer serving plain congee with savory side dishes, while others prefer cooking meats, vegetables and dried goods with rice to create savory or sweet congee. Traditional Cantonese style congee uses long grain rice and is simmered over low heat for at least 1 1/2 hours until the congee is thick and the rice is nearly dissolved. Taiwanese style congee often uses short grain rice with shorter cooking time or just until rice is fully cooked and soft. Usually when the congee is cooked, it will appear soupy; let set for a while to allow the rice to continue to absorb the liquid and expand to become supple.

To enhance the aromas of a savory congee, chopped celery, shredded ginger, and minced green onions or cilantro are sprinkled on top prior to serving. Chinese celery is preferable to regular celery when used to enhance the aroma; hence in this cookbook, celery refers to Chinese celery.

麵的種類五花八門，本書內的麵除了包含由麵粉做成的各種麵條外，還將由米磨成粉做的河粉(粿條) 米粉、年糕，及綠豆粉做的冬粉等歸在麵類，以下將常用的簡述如下：

普通麵條	雞蛋麵	伊麵
以麵粉加水揉製而成，有不同寬、細及乾麵、新鮮麵等多種選擇，是最常見的麵條。無論是湯麵、拌麵、炒麵或燴麵，均可使用此種麵條。地方性小吃通常使用當地特產麵條，但讀者若買不到，皆可用此種普通麵條取代。	是由麵粉和雞蛋為主做成的麵條，顏色偏黃，有寬、細，常用於廣式麵點。	由麵粉和雞蛋為主做成的麵條，先經水煮熟後，再入鍋中油炸定形後出售，通常食之前先煮軟再料理，伊麵被視為速食麵的老祖宗，為廣東人常吃的麵條之一。
Wheat Noodles Made by kneading wheat flour and water, these are the most versatile and common form of noodles, available in various widths and thicknesses; sold either dried or fresh. Whether in *noodle soups, tossed noodles, stir-fried noodles,* or *sauce over noodles,* every regional noodle dish uses its local specialty noodle. When the local style is unavailable, *plain wheat-flour noodles* are always the preferred alternative.	**Egg Noodles** The main ingredients are wheat flour and eggs, resulting in a yellowish noodle. They are made thin or wide and are often used in Cantonese noodle dishes.	**Yee-Fu Noodles** Frequently used in Cantonese noodle dishes, their main ingredients are wheat flour and eggs. Ready-made *Yee-Fu noodles* are first boiled, then deep-fried and molded into shape for packaging. They must be boiled until soft before using. *Instant noodles* are believed to have evolved from *Yee-Fu noodles.*

There are an amazing number of noodle varieties as well as an extraordinary diversity in cooking methods. In addition to a wide range of noodles made from wheat-flour, Asian noodles are made from rice-flour, buckwheat flour, starch of mung beans, as well as additives such as eggs and vegetables. Many Asian noodles have become readily available in most supermarkets; experiment and be adventurous in using the wide selection of Asian noodles. Below are some of the most common types of noodles:

意麵	蔬菜麵	烏龍麵	拉麵
外型捲曲，略帶黃色的薄麵條，為台灣南部特產，適合用來做乾拌麵及湯麵。	以麵粉為主再添加蔬菜汁做成的麵條，不僅顏色漂亮也增加營養價值，如：菠菜麵，或是胡蘿蔔麵。	常見的為白色烏龍麵，一般為經煮熟再冷藏的麵，但也有乾的出售。	傳統的製作方式是用手將麵糰拉甩而成，麵條拉的次數愈多麵愈細，麵條吃起來香Q有嚼勁。市面上有現成的拉麵出售。
E-Mein	**Vegetable Noodles**	**Udon**	**Ramen**
Thin, curly and slightly yellow, *e-mein* are a local specialty of southern Taiwan. They are suitable for *tossed noodle dishes* and *noodle soups.*	Made from wheat flour and vegetable juice, these *vegetable noodles* are not only colorful, but also offer the added nutritional value of ingredients, such as spinach, carrots, etc.	White *udon* is the most common noodle available. Usually pre-boiled and sold refrigerated, they are also available dry and in various shapes and thicknesses--such as round, square and flat.	Traditional handmade *ramen* is made from pulling and separating the dough. The more the dough is tossed and pulled, the thinner and chewier the noodles are. Pre-packaged *ramen* is readily available in most markets.

4   5   6   7

刀削麵	麵疙瘩	油麵	麵線
將麵糰以刀子一片片的削入滾水中煮的稱為刀削麵。在家為了方便可將麵糰略壓成想要的寬度後再切條。這種現做的麵條口感富韌性、有嚼勁。	將麵粉加水和成麵糰,再依想要的大小一片片撕入鍋內煮熟,比拉麵、刀削麵更為簡單,現做現吃,味道鮮美。	淡黃色帶油亮光澤的台式麵條,通常經煮熟拌入油後在市面上出售,有QQ的口感。為台灣人常吃的麵條之一,用於台式炒麵、拌麵或湯麵。	麵線是麵種中最細的,有手工製作及機器製作兩種,常見的為白麵線。傳統麵線在製作時因為拉至數公尺長,在民俗上象徵長壽,常用來當壽麵。白麵線加工蒸過之後即成紅麵線,傳統用於煮蚵仔麵線。

Shaved Noodles

They are made by simultaneously slicing and dropping pieces of dough into boiling water. For convenient home cooking, the dough is rolled into the desired width and thickness then cut into strips. Fresh hand-made shaved noodles are chewy and often cooked *al dente*.

Noodle Pieces

In Chinese, they are literally called *noodle goose bumps*; in theory, they are much like the Italian *orecchiette*, or the Chinese equivalent of *cat ear noodles*. Add water to flour and knead into dough, simultaneously tear off little pieces to the desired size and drop into boiling water. *Noodle pieces* do not have a distinct shape and are easier to make than *ramen* and *shaved noodles*; they are favored for their freshness and interesting variable textures.

Taiwanese Noodles

Generally sold pre-boiled and tossed with oil, they appear light yellow and slippery with an oily sheen. With a chewy texture, *Taiwanese noodles* are one of the most consumed noodles by the Taiwanese, used mostly in Taiwanese style *fried noodles, tossed noodles* and *noodle soups*.

Thin Noodles (Somen)

Available in hand-made and machine-made, these delicate noodles are commonly available in white. Traditional thin noodles are extraordinarily long, reaching several feet and represent the symbol for longevity; often used during birthday celebrations. The brown-colored variety is made by an additional steaming, and is most often used in *Oyster Soup with Thin Noodles*. Since they are much thinner than regular noodles, avoid overcooking as they require very little cooking time, especially with white *somen*.

8

9

10

米粉	河粉	年糕片	冬粉
以尖米為原料製成，有各種不同粗細的米粉，若太大片可剪取所需份量，川燙或浸泡於水中至軟再撈出炒或煮湯。	因不同地區而有不同的名稱，又名粿條或板條，是用粘米粉加水成漿後倒入平盤中蒸熟再切條。可用來做炒河粉或湯河粉。	以米為原料製成，年糕片需冷藏保存，存放越久越乾硬，所以使用前需浸泡於冷水一段時間。炒或煮湯皆適宜。	又稱為粉絲，以綠豆粉做成。使用前浸泡於水中至軟再略剪段使用，吃起來滑嫩爽口。本書湯麵內的麵條大部分可用冬粉取代。

Rice Vermicelli	Fresh Rice Noodles	Rice Cake Slices	Bean Threads
Also known as *mi fen*, are dried and extra thin rice noodles. The main ingredient is long grain rice and is available in various thicknesses. If the pre-packaged *rice vermicelli* is hard to separate, it may be cut with scissors into desired portions. *Rice vermicelli* should be blanched or soaked in hot water until soft, then drained before using in soups or stir-frying.	Depending on the region, they may be called *ho fun* or *rice sticks*. They are made from mixing rice flour and water and placing them in a flat pan to steam until cooked, then cut into strips of various widths. Mostly used for stir-frying or in *noodle soups*.	The main ingredient is rice. *Rice cake slices* should be kept refrigerated, however, the longer they are refrigerated, the harder and dryer they become. They should be softened, by soaking in cold water before using in soups or stir-frying.	Also known as *mung bean noodles* and *cellophane noodles,* are made from the starch of mung beans. Soak in water and cut to small pieces before use. They are favored for their uniquely subtle light flavors and smooth, slippery texture. *Bean threads* can be used instead of noodles for most of the *noodle soup* dishes in this cookbook.

二人份的麵條

本書為了統一份量，所有湯麵、拌麵、炒麵或燴麵皆以450公克的煮熟麵條做為二人食用的標準份量。

乾麵條及新鮮麵條煮熟後的重量差別很大，乾麵條煮熟吸水後重量會增加為原來的三倍左右，而新鮮的麵條煮熟後重量僅增約2倍。讀者若使用與食譜所列不同的麵條，可參考以下原則自行調整麵條的份量：

乾麵150公克(4兩) 或新鮮麵條225公克(6兩)煮熟後約可得熟麵450 公克 (12 兩)。

麵條的煮法

先將麵條放入多量滾水內攪散，再度沸騰後降低火候煮至麵熟撈出。由於麵條種類很多，且寬細厚薄均不相同，可依麵的種類及個人喜好的軟硬程度調整煮麵時間。新鮮麵條與乾麵條均需使用多量的水，以避免煮麵水變濃稠而影響麵條煮好後的口感。

用來炒麵、涼拌麵或兩面黃的麵條可預先煮熟後漂冷水(圖1)，瀝乾水份並拌入少許油挑鬆(圖2)再使用；用來製作湯麵、燴麵或熱拌麵用的麵條宜現煮現用。

Standard Noodle Portion for Two

Whether used for *noodle soups, tossed noodles, stir-fried noodles* or *sauce over noodles*, most regional noodle dishes use specialty noodles specifically from that region. Unless specially mentioned, this cookbook uniformly uses plain wheat flour noodles for dishes that are not identified with any particular region.

Generally, dried and fresh noodles will weigh more after boiling. When cooked, fresh noodles will increase up to twice their original weight, while dried noodles will absorb even more water and triple in original weight. To simplify and standardize portions for the recipes in this cookbook, 1 lb. (450g) of cooked noodles will be used uniformly as a portion for two. When using noodles other than those specified, the following general rule should be applied:

1/3 lb. (150g) of dried noodles and 1/2 lb. (225g) of fresh noodles will yield 1 lb. (450g) of cooked noodles.

Boiling Noodles

Bring a large pot of water to boil, add noodles, and gently stir to separate the noodles. When the water returns to a boil, reduce heat, and continue to cook until done; remove and drain. Since noodles come in various widths and thicknesses, cooking times may vary as well. Adjust the cooking time accordingly, as well as to the individual's preferred firmness.

To prevent sticking, fresh noodles generally contain more loose flour than dried noodles; therefore, a larger amount of water should be used to cook fresh noodles. Too little water will cause the water to become murky and thicken, thus affecting the quality of the noodles.

To prepare stir-fried noodles, cold tossed noodles, pan-fried or fried noodle dishes, noodles should be boiled, drained, and rinsed with cold water (Fig.1) until cool to the touch; drain again thoroughly, then toss noodles with oil (Fig.2); set aside. To prepare noodle soups, sauce over noodles, or hot tossed noodle dishes, noodles should be boiled and served immediately.

麵的吃法與變化

麵的吃法變化多，以下為最常見的。

1. **湯麵** 麵條煮熟後放入已備好的熱湯料內即是湯麵。

2. **燴麵** 將煮好帶有濃稠湯汁的麵料淋在煮好的麵上。

3. **拌麵** 有熱拌及涼拌兩種。熱拌是將麵條煮好後即拌入醬料；涼拌則先將煮熟後的麵條冷藏，食用時再拌入醬料。

4. **炒麵** 將備好的肉、蔬菜、調味料等與煮熟的麵條一起炒拌均勻即為炒麵。

5. **兩面黃** 將雞蛋麵條煮熟後放入油鍋內煎或炸成麵餅狀的兩面黃，再將炒好帶有濃稠湯汁的麵料淋在麵上，是廣東人特殊的料理方式。

■ 以上各種麵類都可與大蒜、生辣椒、辣椒醬、醋及胡椒等配食。此外書內提供的小菜也都是吃麵時的好搭檔。

Variations on Noodle Cooking

There are many ways to cook and enjoy noodles, following are some of the most common:

1. **Noodle Soups** Noodles are boiled, drained, and placed in a large bowl of prepared soup. Usually served piping hot.

2. **Sauce Over Noodles** A prepared thick sauce is poured over cooked noodles.

3. **Tossed Noodles** Served either hot or cold, *hot tossed noodles* require that the noodles be served immediately after boiling and tossed with a prepared sauce. *Cold tossed noodles* require that boiled noodles to be chilled, then tossed with a sauce just prior to serving.

4. **Stir-fried Noodles** Cooked noodles are stir-fried with prepared meats, vegetables and seasonings.

5. **Pan-Fried/Fried Noodles** A uniquely Cantonese style fried noodle dish, literally translated, as "Double-Faced Golden Noodles". *Egg noodles* are boiled, then deep-fried or pan-fried into a large pancake shape, then served with a thick sauce poured over the fried noodles.

■ One will find in most Chinese restaurants or noodle houses a variety of condiments on the table, such as minced garlic, fresh chili peppers, chili pastes, vinegar, and pepper, as they are great complements to any noodle dish. Additionally, side dishes and appetizers included in this cookbook are also frequent and popular companions to any noodle dish.

Frequently Used Oil, Sauces & Pastes

1. 油 傳統中國菜多使用花生油及豬油，可使菜餚散發獨特的油香味。因現代油品種類繁多，所含香味、功能、營養、熱量不一，可依個人喜好選用較清淡的大豆、玉米、葵花油或其他風味的油。現代人為了健康考量，使用橄欖油煮中國菜的人已逐漸增多。

2. 麻油 將芝麻榨油製成。由黑芝麻製成的胡麻油(黑麻油)味道較濃，通常用於特別的菜餚如麻油雞麵線。白芝麻製的麻油(香油)味道較淡，一般烹飪時常滴數滴來增添菜餚香味。

3. 辣油 將熱油倒入粗粒辣椒粉內，再濾除辣椒粉即為簡易辣油。

4. 醬油 由黃豆或黑豆蒸熟發酵製成。醬油種類很多，通常淡色菜餚使用淡色醬油(生抽)較不會影響菜的色澤，需要加深菜餚色澤時可用深色醬油(老抽)，一般烹調可使用普通醬油。醬油膏較一般醬油濃稠，通常用來沾食，本書內使用醬油膏的部分，皆可以普通醬油代替。

5. 醋 醋的種類很多，傳統中國菜多使用由米釀製而成的米醋。米醋分白、烏和紅醋等。書內使用的有白醋和烏醋兩種。一般烹飪及涼拌多使用白米醋，若無可用其他蔬果釀製的白醋代替，烏醋則多用於羹類，可使風味倍增。

6. 米酒 以米釀造而成，用於一般烹飪料理。可去腥味及增添菜餚風味。

7. 辣椒醬、辣豆瓣醬 將辣椒攪碎加鹽即成辣椒醬。若加入蠶豆釀製即為辣豆瓣醬。除當沾料使用外，也可與菜餚一同烹煮，增加辛辣味。

8. 豆瓣醬 由黃豆和麵粉煮熟醱酵製成，有辣及不辣兩種。烹調時，先於油內炒過後再加其他材料，是做炸醬麵、牛肉麵的重要調味料。

9. 沙茶醬 由多種辛香料磨碎調製而成，味稍辣。用來炒肉、炒麵、拌麵及調製火鍋沾料。

10. 甜麵醬 為麵糰醱酵製成，是中國菜上有名的調味醬之一，京醬肉絲及包北平烤鴨餅皮上的醬料，均使用到甜麵醬。

11. 海鮮醬 由麵粉、黃豆、糖及其他辛香料製成的甜味深色醬。可作沾料、醃料、炒及燒烤之用。

12. 芝麻醬 由芝麻加工製成，具濃郁的芝麻香氣，常用於調製涼拌菜及乾拌麵的醬汁上。

1. Oil Traditional Chinese cuisine uses peanut oil or lard primarily, as they impart particular aromas to foods. However, there are a wide variety of edible oils, with varying aromas, functions, nutritional values and caloric contents, that are much preferred by the modern day Chinese chefs. One may choose lighter flavored oils, such as soybean, corn or sunflower oil, etc. Increasingly, olive oil has become popular even for Chinese cuisine, as it is indisputably one of the healthiest edible oils.

2. Sesame Oil An aromatic and robust oil, it is pressed from white or black sesame seeds. *White sesame oil* is rarely used as cooking oil, but is frequently drizzled on food as a seasoning or to enhance the aroma. *Black sesame oil* has a richer and nuttier flavor, and is specifically called for in certain dishes, such as "Sesame Flavored Chicken Somen".

3. Chili Oil Available in most Asian supermarkets, *chili oil* can be made easily by pouring smoking hot oil over coarse chili flakes, then draining to remove the chili flakes.

4. Soy Sauce Made from fermented soybeans or black beans. Soy sauce comes in many styles: *light soy sauce (sen cho)* is used for lighter color dishes; *dark soy sauce (lao cho)* is used to darken the color of a dish; regular soy sauce is most commonly used and is suitable for general cooking. *Soy paste* is thicker than soy sauce and is often used as a dipping sauce. If unavailable, all soy pastes used in this book may be substituted with regular soy sauce.

5. Vinegar Distilled from a variety of sources, Chinese cuisine primarily uses vinegars distilled from rice grains. *Rice vinegars* are available in white, black and red. *White rice vinegar* is used extensively throughout Chinese cooking, especially in salads, pickles and *cold side dishes*, if unavailable; vinegars distilled from fruits may be used. *Black vinegar* is often drizzled on chowders or thickened soups prior to serving.

6. Rice Wine Distilled from rice, it is used throughout Chinese cooking. *Rice wine* functions as a freshener or as an agent to eliminate offensive smells, especially from fish or meats.

7. Chili Paste · Chili Bean Paste Chili paste is a blended paste of crushed peppers and salt. Chili Bean Paste is made from chilies and fava beans. Both pastes may be used interchangeably, either as a dipping sauce, or added to a dish during cooking to increase spiciness.

8. Bean Paste (doban jiang) Made from cooked and fermented soybeans and flour, it is rarely served as a dipping sauce and should be stir-fried in oil before combining with other ingredients. It is an indispensable ingredient in certain dishes, such as "Braised Beef and Noodle Soup" and "Soy Flavored Meat Sauce Over Noodles".

9. Sa-Tsa BBQ Paste A thick and slightly spicy paste, it is a unique blend of a variety of minced herbs and spices. *Sa-Tsa* is used with stir-fried meats, noodles, *tossed noodles*, as well as a dipping sauce for *hot pot* dishes.

10. Sweet Bean Paste (tian mian jiang) Made from fermented flour dough, it is famous in Chinese cuisine and is an indispensable ingredient in making Beijing Sauce as well as a dipping paste when serving "Peking Duck".

11. Hoisin Sauce A dark, sweet and rich sauce made from flour, soybeans, sugar and an assortment of herbs and spices. It can be used as a dipping sauce, marinade, or BBQ sauce.

12. Sesame Paste Made from ground, toasted sesame seeds, with a robust and nutty sesame aroma, it is frequently used in sauces for Chinese salads, *cold side dishes*, or *tossed noodles*.

Frequently Used Spices & Dried Goods

蝦米
即晒乾後的小蝦，使用前略沖水再使用。其味道鮮美，常用來煮湯、炒青菜、炒麵或煮油飯等。

乾辣椒
新鮮辣椒晒乾後即成乾辣椒，常用於辛辣菜餚如宮保雞丁。

油蔥酥
將新鮮紅蔥頭切片後放入油內炒或炸過即為油蔥酥，多用來增添菜餚的香味。市面上有現成的出售，可儲存於冰箱數月。

豆豉
將烏豆蒸熟醱酵，再加鹽水釀製而成，為中國獨特調味材料之一。豆豉具鹹味，常與剁碎的辣椒、薑、蒜等攪拌或炒香再與海鮮或肉類一起烹調。

Dried Shrimp
They are small and sun-dried, and should be rinsed with water before use. With a flavorful taste, they are often used in soups, stir-fried vegetables, fried noodles or glutinous rice.

Dried Chili Peppers
Fresh chili peppers are sun-dried; frequently used in spicy dishes, such as "Kung Pao Chicken".

Fried Shallots
Used to enhance flavor, fresh shallots are sliced then stir-fried or deep-fried. Prepackaged *fried shallots* may be found in most Asian supermarkets, they can be kept fresh for several months in the refrigerator.

Fermented Black Beans
Black soybeans are steamed, fermented, and brined; they are one of the most distinctive ingredients in Chinese cuisine. Used for flavoring, they are salty and are often used in conjunction with minced chili, ginger and garlic, then stir-fried or steamed with seafood or meats.

金針

為晒乾後的萱草花蕾，因花蕾金黃細長，似金色的針故名金針。使用時切去硬蒂頭再用水泡軟。金針營養價值高且滋味鮮美，常做為菜餚配料。

木耳

生長在朽木上的菌類，因其形似耳朵而得名。木耳質地軟但有脆的口感，使用前需泡水去蒂。黑木耳大多用來做菜；白木耳除了做菜之外還可以用來煮甜湯。

香菇

香菇是栽培在木頭上的菌類，除增加菜餚的鮮美外，有肉的口感，是素食者常用的烹飪材料；乾香菇使用前用水泡軟約30分鐘。若急用時可加水蓋過香菇入微波爐內加熱。

蓮子

蓮子為睡蓮科植物的果實。乾蓮子使用前無需泡水，洗淨後可直接烹煮。有些蓮子有添加物，購買時要避免挑選顏色過白的，若察覺有異味，可先不蓋鍋煮，讓氣味揮發後再烹調。蓮子除了煮甜湯以外，也可以與排骨同煮。

Dried Lily Buds

Due to their golden color and slender shape, they are literally named "golden needles" in Chinese. They should be soaked in water and removed of their hard stems before use. *Dried lily buds* are nutritious and have a fresh earthy flavor; they can be used in a variety of dishes.

Dried Wood Ears

Wood ears are "ear-shaped" fungi that grow on decayed wood, hence, named *wood ears*. They are slippery, but have a crispy texture; they should be soaked in water and removed of their stems before use. *Black wood ears* are used mostly in salty dishes, while *white wood ears* can be used in both salty dishes or in sweet desserts.

Chinese Black Mushrooms

Also known as *Shiitake* (in Japanese), these fungi are grown and harvested from hardwood trees, they have a rich and woody flavor and will intensify the flavors of a dish. Because of their meaty texture, they are frequently used as meat substitutes in Chinese vegetarian dishes. Dried mushrooms should be soaked in water to soften for 30 minutes before using. To save soaking time, they can be covered with water and heated in the microwave.

Lotus Seeds

The dried seeds of a *Nymphaeaceae* plant, (commonly known as *lotus*), should be rinsed prior to use, (soaking in water is unnecessary). Avoid the ultra white seeds, as they may be bleached with hydrogen peroxide; when a slight odor is detected during cooking, boil them without the lid, until the odor is disbursed. *Lotus seeds* are often used in sweet desserts, as well as in chicken or pork rib soups.

常用香料及乾貨

Frequently Used Spices & Dried Goods

芝麻	柴魚片	胡椒	五香粉
市售有黑色及白色的生芝麻與炒熟的芝麻。將生芝麻放入乾淨鍋內，以中火炒數分鐘即為熟芝麻，多用於撒在菜餚上以增加香味或攪碎煮甜湯。	將鰹魚蒸熟後晒乾成柴魚乾，再刨成薄片裝袋銷售，可撒在菜餚上食用或用來煮高湯。	因胡椒粒成熟度不同而有不同顏色，常用的為磨碎的黑胡椒及白胡椒，其辛辣程度及香氣不同，皆用來增添食物的風味，一般視菜餚顏色或個人喜好使用。	由五種以上的香料如八角、花椒、桂皮、陳皮、丁香、茴香等研磨而成粉狀，有特殊的香味，為中菜烹調上常用的香料之一。
Sesame Seeds Available in black or white; raw or roasted, roasted *sesame seeds* can be made by stir-frying raw seeds in a clean and dry frying pan, over medium heat for a few minutes until fragrant. Mostly used to sprinkle on salads or certain dishes, or finely ground to make sweet dessert soups.	**Bonito Shavings** A type of fish, similar to tuna or mackerel, bonito is steamed, sun-dried, then shredded into paper-thin slices before packaging. They can be sprinkled on food or used to make soup stock.	**Pepper** Pepper-corns vary in color depending on their ripeness. The most frequently used are ground *black* and *white peppers*. They vary slightly in spiciness and aroma, both are used to add a pungent flavor; use either black or white as desired.	**Five Spice Powder** Mixed and ground to a fine powder, although named *five spice powder*, it contains more than five spices, including *star anise, Szechwan peppercorns, cinnamon, dried orange peels, cloves, fennel seeds*, etc. With a distinct aroma, it is one of the frequently used seasonings in Chinese cuisine.

9   10   11   12

13 | 14 | 15 | 16

花椒粉	椒鹽	八角	玉米粉
將花椒粒乾炒數分鍾待冷再磨或搗成粉。花椒粒又稱山椒或川椒，市面有賣現成的。	將1大匙鹽炒熱再與1/2小匙的胡椒粉或花椒粉混合，可當沾料使用。	為植物的果實，果殼有八個角，故稱八角，是香料的一種。也是五香粉中重要材料之一。	白色粉狀，用來勾芡或醃拌沾裹肉類，以增加嫩度。若無玉米粉可以太白粉取代。

Szechwan Pepper Powder	**Pepper Salt**	**Star Anise**	**Cornstarch**
Also known as "anise pepper". In addition to being peppery and pungent, a numbing aftertaste is its unique characteristic. To make *Szechwan pepper powder*, stir-fry *Szechwan peppercorns* without oil for a few minutes; set aside until cool, then grind or crush to a powder.	Stir-fry 1 T. of salt until hot, then add 1/2 t. of pepper or *Szechwan pepper powder* to mix well, *pepper salt* is used mostly as a dry rub or as a dipping condiment.	The fruit of an evergreen tree, shaped like an 8-pointed star. It is literally named "8-point" in Chinese. It is one of the most well known Chinese herbs, as well as an important ingredient in *five spice powder*.	This white powder is used to thicken sauces, or to coat, marinate and tenderize meats.

量器 *Measuring Tools*

量調味料時，請用標準量器。所有食譜內的材料，除有特別指示外，均為洗過、削皮後或處理過的淨重。

Use proper measuring tools to ensure accuracy of amounts of ingredients used. Unless specified, all ingredients listed in recipes are washed, peeled, or otherwise prepared to yield net weights.

1杯(1飯碗)=16大匙 1 c. (1 cup) = 236 c.c.	1大匙(1湯匙) 1 T. (1 Tablespoon) = 15 c.c.	1小匙(1茶匙) 1 t. (1 teaspoon) = 5 c.c.

蔬菜種類繁多，在不影響風味的情況下大部份食譜中的蔬菜是可替換的，讀者可依季節特性、市場價格及個人喜好選用。

There are many types of vegetables available, and most of the vegetables in this cookbook are interchangeable. Readers can pick and choose based on the current season and personal preference.

小黃瓜
Japanese Cucumbers

苦瓜
Bitter Melons

Asian

雪豆
Snow Peas

豆芽菜
Bean Sprouts

洋菇
Mushrooms

柳
Clamshe.

大白菜
Napa Cabbage

小白菜
Short Bok Choy

青江菜
Bok Choy

芥蘭菜
Chinese Broccoli

Wate

老薑／嫩薑
Ginger/Baby Ginger Roots

蒜頭
Garlic Gloves

蒜苗
Fresh Garlic Spears

香菜
Cilantro

紅
S

青椒/甜椒 (紅、黃或橘)
Bell Peppers

白蘿蔔
White Radish

馬鈴薯
Potatoes

甜豆
Sweet Peas

四季豆
String Beans

酪梨
Avocado

花椰菜
Cauliflower

青花菜
Broccoli

西洋芹菜
Celery

高麗菜
Cabbage

茼蒿菜
Tong Ho

油菜
Rape Greens (Yau Choy)

菠菜
Spinach

韭黃/韭菜
Chinese Chives/ Leeks

蔥
Green Onions

九層塔
Basil

紅辣椒
Red Chili Peppers

蘆筍
Asparagus

筍絲
Bamboo Shoots

玉米筍
Baby Corns

處理肉及蔬菜

Preparing Meats & Vegetables

家庭烹飪方法有時與餐飲店不太相同，特別提出以下技巧，希望能幫助讀者做出色香味俱全的美味佳餚。

肉的切法

用來炒或煮湯的肉絲或肉片一般多使用上等的里肌肉，但也可以用其它部位的全瘦肉來做。大塊肉在半凍過的情形下較容易切出厚薄一致的肉片或肉絲。忙碌的人則可在超市購買已切好的肉片或肉絲以節省時間。

肉的調味

肉片或肉絲一般以酒、醬油、鹽及玉米粉等來調味，也可多加入蛋白醃一段時間使肉更滑嫩。冷凍肉片或肉絲需先解凍，若有太多水份可略拭乾(圖1)後再調味。有些菜餚特地強調肉的乾香或原味，就不一定要調味，可選帶有少許肥肉的部位較好吃。

炒肉的技巧

先將鍋燒熱，放入少量油轉動一下鍋子使油面擴大，把肉散撒在鍋面(圖2)，待肉的邊緣變色之後才開始翻炒(圖3)。因家庭用的鍋爐火力小，太早翻動易出水成糊狀。炒肉時份量一次不要太多，少油時，使用不沾鍋較簡便易於操作。

Home cooking requires different cooking techniques from those employed in restaurants. This cookbook focuses on simple and easy steps and offers the following tips to enable any cook to prepare delicious, beautiful, and aromatic dishes.

Cutting Meat

Sliced or shredded tenderloin is most commonly used in stir-frying dishes or cooking soup. If not available, other cuts of lean meat may be used. Partially frozen meat pieces will make slicing and shredding easier. Ready-made sliced meat or shredded meat can be purchased in markets.

Seasoning Meat

Sliced or shredded meat is customarily seasoned with cooking wine, soy sauce, salt, and cornstarch. Adding egg white to the meat and refrigerating for several hours will further soften it. Frozen meat should be thawed first; and excess water pat-dried from the meat (Fig.1) prior to seasoning. Some dishes call for the simple tastiness of meat and do not require seasoning in advance. If meat has no seasoning, it is best to use meat that contains a little fat.

Stir-frying Meat

Heat frying pan or wok, put in a few tablespoons of cooking oil and gently move the pan side-to-side so that the oil covers the surface of the pan. Scatter the meat into the pan (Fig.2) and wait until the edges change color before turning the meat to cook the other side (Fig.3). If the stove's heat output is weak or low, turning the meat too soon will release excess meat juices rendering it mushy. Refrain from stir-frying a large quantity of meat at one time to have the best results. Non-stick frying pans are highly suitable for stir-frying since they require less oil.

Stir-frying Vegetables

Any of the following stir-frying techniques will bring about delicious, emerald-green vegetables:

1. Traditional stir-frying of vegetables requires high heat. After the oil is heated, put the

炒青菜的技巧

以下任何方式，皆可炒出翠綠可口的青菜：

1. 傳統炒青菜時火力要大，油燒熱後才放入青菜，隨著水爆聲，即加入約兩大匙的水及調味料快速炒勻，這樣炒出來的蔬菜青脆好吃。

2. 若爐子火力不大，可於加入青菜及水之後蓋鍋燜至水蒸汽冒出，調好味立即翻拌鏟出，效果一樣好。

3. 最簡便的方法是利用微波爐，把青菜放入容器內，加入少許的油、水及調味料，蓋上保鮮膜，加熱2~3分鐘後取出，在原容器內翻拌均勻即可，此法做出來的青菜同樣青脆好吃。本書的米麵簡餐內所搭配的蔬菜若需要事先炒過，都可以用此方式處理。

vegetables into the pan. Water droplets from the vegetables sizzling in the pan will cause minor explosive sounds. Immediately add two tablespoons of water and seasoning and stir-fry quickly; remove. Such a technique allows for crunchy, tasty stir-fried vegetables.

2. If the stove's heat output is weak or low, cover vegetables and water until steam escapes. Add seasoning, blend with the vegetables, and immediately remove from the pan. The results are equally satisfying.

3. The easiest technique is to use the microwave oven. Place vegetables in a microwavable container, add a little oil, water, and seasoning. Cover and cook for 2-3 minutes then remove from the microwave oven; mix the contents well and serve. This technique also yields crunchy, delicious, lush green vegetables. If the rice and noodle recipes in this cookbook call for accompanying stir-fried vegetables, the above technique serves well.

高湯 *Stock*

高湯除用來煮湯外也適合用來烹煮各類菜餚，以提昇美味。

雞肉、雞骨或豬骨...2斤4兩(1350公克)

將材料剁塊，放入滾水內川燙撈出，再隨意加蔥、薑、酒與20杯水燒開，並撈出浮在水面上的泡沫，改以小火蓋鍋煮2~3小時後，將骨頭與雜質撈出過濾，若不喜歡油脂，將高湯置於冰箱中過夜，再把凝固的浮油去除，即可得高湯約10杯。

為簡化烹飪過程，本書湯麵內所用高湯多數使用有調味的罐頭雞湯，2人份湯麵所用的湯份量為5杯，即1罐雞湯加入3杯水。讀者若使用自製高湯取代書內的罐頭雞湯時，可用5杯自製高湯加入⅓小匙的鹽的取代，鹹度可依個人喜好增減。

Stock is used in soups and various dishes to enhance flavor.

Chicken, chicken or pork bones … 3 lbs. (1350g)

Cut ingredients into chunks and blanch in boiling water; remove. Add green onions, ginger root and cooking wine with 20 cups of water to the chunks; bring to boil. Skim the foam from stock; reduce heat to low. Cover and simmer for 2-3 hours. Remove meat and bones; strain to yield about 10 cups. If reduction of grease is desired, refrigerate stock overnight; skim grease from top of stock.

To make quick meals, canned chicken broth is often used in this cookbook to replace stock. Noodle soups for two require a total of 5 cups of stock, or the equivalent of one can of chicken broth mixed with three cups of water. Readers who prefer homemade stock may substitute five cups for the canned variety and add ⅓ teaspoon salt to taste.

罐頭雞湯 *Canned Chicken Broth*

本食譜內使用的罐頭雞湯一罐為408公克(14.5oz)，約2杯，罐上標示一杯的含鹽量為960mg。

Recipes in this cookbook use canned chicken broth weighing 14.5oz (408g), which is approximately 2 cups. Salt content per can is 960mg.

米

RICE 麺 小菜

CHINESE 麺

NOODLES APPETIZERS

簡 SOUPS

SWEETS 湯

餐 甜點

宮保雞丁飯　KUNG PAO CHICKEN OVER RICE

[四川菜]　　　　　　[2人份]

[SZECHWAN CUISINE]　　　　　[SERVES 2]

雞肉...300公克(8兩)

2/3 lb. (300g) boneless chicken

1
醬油、酒...各2/3大匙
玉米粉...1大匙

1
2/3 T. ea.: soy sauce, cooking wine
1 T. cornstarch

乾辣椒...12段

12 pieces dried chili peppers

2
水、醬油...各2大匙
糖...2小匙
醋、玉米粉...各1小匙
麻油...1/2小匙

2
2 T. ea.: water, soy sauce
2 t. sugar
1 t. ea.: vinegar, cornstarch
1/2 t. sesame oil

3
蔥段...1/2杯
去皮花生...4大匙

3
1/2 c. chopped green onions
4 T. roasted peanuts

飯...2碗

2 c. cooked rice

1　雞肉攤開在肉面上略劃刀，或用刀角略剁以使入味，再切粗丁，加**1**料調勻，炒前再拌入1大匙油則肉易炒散開。**2**料調勻置碗內備用。

2　油1大匙與乾辣椒同時放入鍋內，待辣椒炒至呈深褐色，隨將雞肉煎炒開至變色，再加**2**料炒拌均勻後加**3**料略拌即可與飯配食。

■　傳說清末大官丁寶楨常請家廚以炒雞丁宴客，後來到了四川，他的家廚結合當地食辣的口味而加以改良，結果大受歡迎。因丁寶楨曾被封為太子少保（尊稱宮保），故此道菜命名為"宮保雞丁"。

1　Lay chicken flat and lightly score the meat or pound the chicken with a mallet or the edge of a cleaver to absorb marinade easier. Cut the chicken in pieces and mix with **1**. Stir in 1 T. of oil just before stir-frying to help separate the meat during stir-frying. Mix **2** well in a bowl and set aside.

2　Stir-fry chili peppers in 1 T. oil until dark brown. Add chicken and fry until cooked. Put in **2** and mix well. Add **3**; stir briefly then serve with rice.

■　In the palace of a waning Qing Dynasty, the royal tutor Ding Bao Zhen often ordered his house chef to prepare stir-fried chicken for his guests. After arriving in Szechwan, his house chef adapted the local chili-spices to his favorite stir-fried chicken. The result was exuberantly welcomed. Legend has it that when Ding Bao Zhen was promoted to the rank of "Kung Pao" (Royal Teacher to the Prince), the locals began naming this very popular chicken dish after the honorific name of Ding's new title, hence the name "Kung-Pao Chicken."

宮保醬 的最大特色是以乾辣椒放入低溫的油內慢炒，使辣味滲入油內，再以深色、略帶甜酸的**2**料綜合調味汁烹調而成的。拌炒之後的肉丁除了香辣之外還略帶少許的甜酸味。宮保醬除用來炒雞丁外也常用來炒蝦仁及魷魚。

KUNG PAO SAUCE is well known for its spicy flavor which comes from slow cooking the dried chili peppers in oil over low heat. Cooking with the sweet and sour mixture **2**, the cooked meat will have a sweet and tangy taste and a spicy aroma. Kung Pao sauce is also popular in cooking with shrimp and squid.

左宗棠雞飯　GENERAL TSO'S CHICKEN ON RICE

【 湖南菜 】　　　　　【 2人份 】

雞肉...300公克(8兩)

1
- 醬油...⅔大匙
- 蛋白...½個
- 玉米粉...4大匙

蒜、薑末...各2大匙

紅辣椒或紅椒...12片

2
- 水...6大匙
- 醬油...3大匙
- 糖...1大匙
- 醋、玉米粉...各1½小匙

飯...2碗

1　雞肉切粗條，將①料依序調入拌勻。

2　炸油燒熱，將雞肉一條一條放入炸3分鐘，至表面呈金黃色撈出。

3　油2大匙燒熱，先炒香蒜、薑，再略炒紅辣椒，隨即放入②料燒開，加入炸好的雞肉翻拌均勻即成，與飯配食。

■　傳統的做法以帶皮雞肉切粗丁，以過油或炒的方式處理，但目前餐廳則大多炸過再調理，變通法可煎過後再調理的效果也不錯。

■　左宗棠雞是湖南菜中的名菜，可與川菜中的宮保雞丁媲美。相傳是清末名將左宗棠最喜歡的菜餚，每回打勝仗必以此佳餚犒賞將士官兵，因此又稱為左將軍雞或左公雞！

【 HUNAN CUISINE 】　　　　　【 SERVES 2 】

⅔ lb. (300g) boneless chicken

1
- ⅔ T. soy sauce
- ½ egg white
- 4 T. cornstarch

2 T. ea. (minced): garlic, ginger root

12 slices red chili peppers or red bell peppers

2
- 6 T. water
- 3 T. soy sauce
- 1 T. sugar
- 1½ t. ea.: vinegar, cornstarch

2 c. cooked rice

1　Cut chicken into thick strips; add ① in the order listed and mix well.

2　Heat oil for deep-frying then put in chicken strips one by one and fry for 3 minutes until golden brown; remove the chicken.

3　Heat 2 T. oil and stir-fry garlic and ginger until fragrant; add the red chili peppers and stir briefly. Add ② and bring to a boil. Return cooked chicken to pan and mix well; serve with rice.

■　Traditionally this dish is made with stir-fried chicken with skin, but currently most restaurants will deep-fry the chicken strips first. Pan-fried is another popular cooking method.

■　This is famous Hunan cuisine; its popularity matches the "Kung Pao Chicken" in Szechwan cuisine. According to history, this dish was General Tso's favorite dish. Every time he won a battle, his soldiers were rewarded with this dish, hence the name "General Tso's Chicken".

蔥爆牛肉飯

[2人份]

	牛肉片...225公克(6兩)
	蔥段...1杯
1	洋菇片、筍片...共150公克 (4兩)
	醬油...3大匙
2	糖...1大匙
	酒...1大匙
	飯...2碗

1　買來的牛肉片若太大，可切半使用。

2　油1大匙燒熱，先將蔥白爆香再將1料略炒盛出。

3　油3大匙燒熱，放入牛肉片炒開至變色後，入拌勻的2料炒拌，再加炒好的1料及蔥綠炒拌均勻，與飯配食。

■　帶少許肥肉的牛肉片比較嫩，若是全瘦的可加少許玉米粉，可增加肉的嫩度。簡易的蔥爆牛肉，僅用牛肉及蔥，不加洋菇及筍。

SAUTÉED BEEF AND GREEN ONIONS OVER RICE

[SERVES 2]

	½ lb. (225g) beef slices
	1 c. chopped green onions
1	⅓ lb. (150g) total (sliced): mushrooms, bamboo shoots
	3 T. soy sauce
2	1 T. sugar
	1 T. cooking wine
	2 c. cooked rice

1　Cut beef slices in half if too large.

2　Heat 1 T. of oil and stir-fry the white part of the green onion until fragrant; add 1 to stir-fry briefly then remove.

3　Heat 3 T. of oil and stir-fry beef until color changes. Add mixed 2 and stir-fry briefly; add 1 and the green part of the green onions then mix well. Serve with rice.

■ Beef slices with fat are more tender; however, adding a little cornstarch to lean meat will increase tenderness. An easier version of this dish only uses green onions and beef; mushrooms and bamboo shoots may be omitted.

黑胡椒牛柳飯

【 2人份 】

牛排肉...225公克(6兩)	
1	醬油、酒...各⅔大匙
	玉米粉...1大匙
2	青椒絲、洋蔥絲...共225公克(6兩)
3	薑絲、蒜末...各1大匙
4	鹽...¼小匙，黑胡椒...½小匙
	辣醬油...2大匙，玉米粉...1小匙
	水...3大匙
	飯...2碗

1　牛肉切長條狀醃入1料，炒前拌油1大匙則炒時肉較易分開。

2　油1大匙燒熱，入2料略炒撈出，餘汁不要並擦乾鍋面。

3　油2大匙燒熱，炒香3料，入牛肉炒至變色，隨入2料及拌勻的4料炒勻即可與飯配食。

黑胡椒汁 是現代流行的中西混合味，其特色是以多量黑胡椒及辣醬油調製而成(見4料)。除有名的黑胡椒牛柳之外，還可用來炒肉丁、肉片、焗肉排，用途廣泛。

BEEF AND BLACK PEPPER SAUCE OVER RICE

[SERVES 2]

½ lb. (225g) beef fillet	
1	⅔ T. ea.: soy sauce, cooking wine
	1 T. cornstarch
2	½ lb (225g) ea. (shredded): green bell peppers, onions
3	1 T. ea. (minced): garlic, ginger root
4	¼ t. salt; ½ t. black pepper
	2 T. Worcestershire sauce
	1 t. cornstarch; 3 T. water
	2 c. cooked rice

1　Cut beef in strips and mix with 1. Just before stir-frying, stir in 1 T. of oil to help separate the meat during stir-frying.

2　Heat 1 T. of oil to stir-fry 2 briefly; remove. Discard remaining sauce and wipe the surface of the wok dry.

3　Heat 2 T. of oil and stir in 3 until fragrant. Stir-fry beef until color changes; add in 2 and mixed 4 then mix well. Serve with rice.

BLACK PEPPER SAUCE　(as in 4) is a popular fusion sauce that is often used in many dishes. Its uniqueness comes from large quantities of black pepper and Worcestershire sauce. This sauce is also great for baked chops, stir-frying diced and sliced meat.

蠔油牛肉飯　BEEF WITH OYSTER SAUCE OVER RICE

【 廣東菜 】　　　　　【 2人份 】

牛肉片...225公克(6兩)

① 醬油、酒...各⅔大匙
玉米粉...1大匙

② 蔥白...6段
薑...6片
甜椒片...隨意

③ 水...½杯
蠔油、醬油...各1大匙
玉米粉...2小匙
糖...¾小匙
麻油、胡椒...各少許

芥蘭菜(或其他蔬菜)...225公克(6兩)
飯...2碗

1 牛肉片(圖1)加①料拌勻，炒前先拌入1大匙油炒時肉較易炒開，芥蘭菜略川燙後沖冷水並瀝乾水份備用。

2 油3大匙燒熱，炒香②料續入肉片半煎炒開至肉變色後，加拌勻的③料攪拌煮開，再入芥蘭菜炒勻即可燴在飯或麵上。。

■ 以蠔油為主調成的③料綜合調味汁，用來烹調海鮮、肉類、蔬菜等都很適合，使用少量的蠔油即能帶出食物本身的鮮味，普遍用於廣東菜，有名的菜餚有蠔油鮑魚片、蠔油生菜等。

【 CANTONESE CUISINE 】　　　　【 SERVES 2 】

½ lb. (225g) beef slices

① ⅔ T. ea.: soy sauce, cooking wine
1 T. cornstarch

② 6 pieces white part of green onions
6 slices ginger root
red and yellow bell pepper slices as desired

③ ½ c. water
1 T. ea.: oyster sauce, soy sauce
2 t. cornstarch; ¾ t. sugar
dash of sesame oil & pepper

½ lb. (225g) Chinese Broccoli (or other green leafy vegetable)

2 c. cooked rice

1 Add ① to beef slices (Fig. 1) and mix well. Stir in 1 T. of oil just before stir-frying to help separate the meat during stir-frying. Blanch the Chinese broccoli in hot water and rinse with cold water; remove and set aside.

2 Heat 3 T. oil, stir-fry ② until fragrant, add beef and stir-fry until color changes. Pour in mixed ③; mix well and bring to a boil. Mix in Chinese Broccoli, then pour over cooked rice. Serve.

■ Mixed sauce ③ is mainly made of oyster sauce. This sauce is perfect for cooking seafood, meats and vegetables. Using just a small amount will bring out the natural flavor of the ingredients. Oyster sauce is frequently used in Cantonese cuisine. Some famous dishes include "Sliced Abalone in Oyster Sauce" and "Lettuce in Oyster Sauce".

糖醋肉飯　SWEET AND SOUR PORK ON RICE

【 廣東菜 】	【 2人份 】
瘦肉(豬、牛或雞)...225公克(6兩)	

① 醬油...⅔大匙
　 蛋(打散)...1個
　 玉米粉...6大匙

② 洋蔥、鳳梨、青椒或甜椒
　　　...切塊共2杯

　 蒜末...1小匙

③ 糖、醋、水...各3大匙
　 番茄醬...2大匙
　 鹽...½小匙
　 玉米粉...1½大匙

　 飯...2碗

1　肉切2公分厚片、兩面捶鬆，切成塊狀，加①料拌勻後，與玉米粉裝入袋內翻滾，使均勻裹上粉。

2　炸油3杯燒熱，將肉逐塊全部放入，炸約4分鐘至表面酥脆至肉熟撈出。

3　油1大匙燒熱，將②料略炒鏟出；擦乾鍋面，油2大匙燒熱，炒香蒜末，隨入調勻的③料攪拌燒開，再放回肉塊及②料炒拌均勻與飯配食。

■　廣東泡菜（見137頁）清脆酸甜可取代②料來煮糖醋肉。

[CANTONESE CUISINE]	[SERVES 2]
½ lb. (225g) lean pork, beef or chicken	

① ⅔ T. soy sauce
　 1 egg, beaten
　 6 T. cornstarch

② 2 c. total (cut in pieces): onions, pineapple or bell
　　 peppers

　 1 t. minced garlic

③ 3 T. ea.: sugar, vinegar, water
　 2 T. ketchup
　 ½ t. salt
　 1½ T. cornstarch

　 2 c. cooked rice

1　Slice beef to about 1" (2 cm) thick, pound the meat to tenderize then cut it into pieces. Add ① and mix well. Put the cornstarch in a bag ; add the meat then shake it to coat the meat evenly.

2　Heat 3 c. oil for deep-frying, put meat in slowly. Fry for about 4 minutes until surface is crispy and meat is cooked. Remove.

3　Heat 1 T. oil, stir-fry ② briefly and remove. Wipe surface of the wok dry. Heat 2 T. oil to stir-fry garlic until fragrant. Add mixed ③, mix well and bring to a boil. Add meat and ②; mix well and serve with rice.

■　"Cantonese Pickled Salad" (see P.137) is a light and crunchy, sweet and sour dish; it is suitable to use as a replacement of ②.

糖醋汁　是以糖、醋、番茄醬為主調成(如③料)，適宜喜歡甜酸口味者。糖醋料理的製作是將材料酥炸或煎過後，淋或拌上糖醋汁而成；餐館中受歡迎的甜酸肉及糖醋魚即為糖醋風味菜。

SWEET AND SOUR SAUCE (as in ③) is mainly made of sugar, vinegar and ketchup. It is ideal for people who like sweet and tangy flavors. Sweet and sour dishes are usually made with ingredients deep-fried or pan-fried then drizzled or mixed with sweet and sour sauce. This sauce is used to make the popular "Sweet and Sour Pork" dish.

京醬肉末飯

【 2人份 】

	絞肉(豬、牛或雞)...225公克(6兩)
	洋蔥末...½杯
①	冷凍或新鮮蔬菜丁...共1½杯
	醬油...2大匙
	水、甜麵醬...各1大匙
②	酒、糖...各½大匙
	玉米粉、麻油...各1小匙
	飯...2碗

1 將①料略沖水瀝乾，微波加熱3
   分鐘備用。

2 油3大匙燒熱，先炒香洋蔥，
   再入絞肉炒開至變色，隨入②
   料拌勻，最後放入①料炒勻與
   飯配食。

京醬 是以甜麵醬為主調成(如
②料)，常使用於傳統的北方風
味菜餚，如京醬肉絲、醬爆蟹
等，馳名中外的北平烤鴨是將
薄餅塗京醬後再包裹烤鴨及京
蔥食用。

GROUND PORK WITH BEIJING SAUCE OVER RICE
【 BEIJING CUISINE 】

【 SERVES 2 】

	½ lb. (225g) ground pork, beef or chicken
	½ c. minced onions
①	**1½ c. total (diced): frozen or fresh vegetables**
	2 T. soy sauce
	1 T. ea.: water, sweet bean paste
②	**½ T. ea.: cooking wine, sugar**
	1t. ea.: cornstarch, sesame oil
	2 c. cooked rice

1 Rinse ① and drain. Microwave for 3 minutes and set aside.

2 Heat 3 T of oil and stir-fry onions until fragrant. Add the ground
   meat; stir-fry until color changes. Add ② and mix well. Return ①
   to the pan; mix well. Serve with rice.

BEIJING SAUCE (as in ②) is a
mixture mainly made from
sweet bean paste. It is often
used in traditional Northern
Chinese dishes such as "Crab
with Beijing Sauce". The
famous "Beijing Roasted Duck"
dish is served with slices of
duck, green onions and Beijing
Sauce all wrapped in a flour
tortilla.

洋蔥茄汁排骨飯

豬排或牛排2片...300公克 (8兩)

1
- 醬油、玉米粉...各1大匙
- 酒...1大匙

2
- 洋蔥絲...1杯
- 紅辣椒絲、薑絲...共2大匙

3
- 水...½杯
- 醬油...3大匙
- 糖、醋、番茄醬...各1½大匙
- 玉米粉...½大匙

飯...2碗

1　肉排去肥肉用刀背或捶肉器捶鬆，肉邊的筋略切以免收縮，加1料調勻。

2　油2大匙燒熱，將肉排兩面煎至金黃色 (每面煎約1分半鐘)，肉熟鏟出。

3　另加油1大匙，將2料炒香，再入調勻的3料燒開，放回肉排炒拌均勻與飯配食。

茄汁　是用洋蔥及3料烹調而成。茄汁的糖醋味比廣東式的糖醋汁味淡，常用於烹煮牛柳及魚片等。除洋蔥外可隨意加青豆或菇類。

PORK CHOPS WITH KETCHUP SAUCE ON RICE

【 SERVES 2 】

2 pork chops or steak, ⅔ lb. (300g)

1
- 1 T. ea.: soy sauce, cornstarch
- 1 T. cooking wine

2
- 1 c. shredded onions
- 2 T. total (shredded): red chili peppers, ginger root

3
- ½ c. water; 3 T. soy sauce; ½ T. cornstarch
- 1½ T. ea.: sugar, vinegar, ketchup

2 c. cooked rice

1　Remove fat from meat and tenderize with a mallet; make several cuts on outside tendons to keep it from curling. Mix with 1 to coat evenly.

2　Heat 2 T. oil, fry meat 1½ minutes on each side until both sides are golden brown. Remove meat and set aside.

3　Heat 1 T. oil and stir-fry 2 until fragrant; add mixture 3 and heat until bubbly. Return meat to wok and stir to mix well. Serve with rice.

KETCHUP SAUCE used in this recipe is made from mixture 3 and onions. This sweet and tangy flavor is milder than the Cantonese sweet and sour sauce and is often used to cook beef and fish filets. Green peas and mushrooms can be added as desired.

[四川菜]	[2人份]	[SZECHWAN CUISINE]	[SERVES 2]

蝦仁*...300公克(8兩)

2/3 lb. (300g) shelled shrimp*

1
鹽...1/4小匙
酒...1小匙
玉米粉...2小匙

1
1/4 t. salt
1 t. cooking wine
2 t. cornstarch

2
蒜末、薑末...各1大匙
洋蔥(切碎)、青豆...共1/2杯

2
1 T. ea. (minced): garlic, ginger root
1/2 c. total: green peas and chopped onions

3
番茄醬...3大匙
酒釀**(圖1)或酒...1大匙
辣豆瓣醬...1小匙

3
3 T. ketchup
1 T. fermented wine rice** (Fig. 1) or cooking wine
1 t. chili bean paste

4
水...1/2杯
鹽...1/2小匙
糖...2/3大匙
玉米粉...1/2大匙

4
1/2 c. water
1/2 t. salt
2/3 T. sugar
1/2 T. cornstarch

飯...2碗

2 c. cooked rice

1 蝦仁拌入①料，將③及④料分別調好備用。

1 Marinate shrimp in ①. Mix ③ and ④ separately; set aside.

2 油3大匙燒熱，將蝦仁炒開至變色撈出，油2大匙將②料依序放入炒香，隨入③料爆香，加④料攪開成濃汁，再加入炒好的蝦仁，可隨意撒上松子，即可與飯配食。

2 Heat 3 T. oil, stir-fry shrimp until separated and color changes; remove. Heat 2 T. oil, stir-fry ② in the order listed, until fragrant. Add ③ and stir until bubbles appear; add mixture ④. Cook and stir until thickened. Return shrimp to wok. Pine nuts may be added as desired. Serve with rice.

* 蝦仁用牙籤挑除腸泥(若用大蝦仁則用刀片開成兩片，取出腸泥後，加1小匙的鹽及1大匙的水，輕輕抓拌，用清水沖洗瀝乾並拭乾水份即可用。

* Use a toothpick to devein the shrimp. (Use a knife to cut through and devein if large shrimp are used.) Add 1 t. of salt and 1 T. of water, mix lightly, rinse, drain and pat dry.

** 酒釀即糯米飯加糖及酒麴發酵製成。

** Fermented wine rice is made from fermenting glutinous rice with sugar and wine. It may be found in the oriental food section at supermarkets.

乾燒醬 是以②、③及④料烹調而成。其特色是使用多量的蔥(或洋蔥)、蒜、薑等香辛料以及番茄醬、酒釀、辣豆瓣醬等調味料，是四川常用的調味汁。多用來烹煮蝦、魚及鮮貝等。

SPICY KETCHUP SAUCE is made of mixtures ②, ③ and ④. This sauce uses a lot of green onions (or onions), garlic, ginger, ketchup, fermented wine rice, spicy bean paste and other herbs and spices. This is a common Szechwan sauce and is often used to cook shrimp, fish and scallops.

【 台灣菜 】		【 2人份 】
雞腿或雞半隻...600公克(1斤)		
麻油...4大匙		
①	薑...12片	
	乾辣椒...6段	
②	酒、醬油...各4大匙	
	水...½杯	
	糖...½大匙	
③	冬粉...1束(42公克)	
	九層塔...1杯	
	飯...2碗	

1 雞剁塊備用。冬粉泡軟瀝乾。

2 麻油4大匙燒熱，以小火炒香①料至薑片呈金黃色，改大火隨入雞塊煎約5分鐘至兩面呈金黃色，將②料依序放入燒開，改中火蓋鍋燒煮15分鐘(中途需翻拌)，再加③料炒至汁快收乾時即可與飯配食。

[**TAIWANESE CUISINE**]		[**SERVES 2**]
1⅓ lbs. (600g) chicken or chicken thighs		
4 T. sesame oil		
①	12 slices ginger root	
	6 dried chili peppers	
②	4 T. ea.: cooking wine, soy sauce	
	½ c. water	
	½ T. sugar	
③	1 bunch of packaged bean threads, 1.5 oz (42g)	
	1 c. basil	
	2 c. cooked rice	

1 Wash chicken and pat dry. Cut into pieces. Soak the bean threads in water until soft; drain.

2 Heat 4 T. sesame oil, stir-fry ① over low heat until ginger turns a golden color. Turn heat to high and fry chicken for 5 minutes, until both sides are golden brown. Add ② in the order listed; bring to a boil. Cover and cook over medium heat 15 minutes; stir occasionally during cooking. Add ③ and stir-fry until liquid is almost evaporated. Serve with rice.

三杯 的調味標準是使用同等份量的麻油、米酒、醬油來烹調，其特色是以多量的麻油與薑片炒出香味，起鍋前再加入九層塔提香。除常見的三杯雞外，小卷、肥腸、魚肚也是著名的三杯風味菜。

THREE SAUCES refers to equal portions of sesame oil, rice wine, and soy sauce. The uniqueness of this dish is the stir-frying of the ginger root in a lot of sesame oil which brings out the special flavor. Fresh basil is added at the end to enhance that flavor. Squid may be used instead of chicken to make another popular Taiwanese "Three Sauce" dish.

魚香茄子飯

【 2人份 】

| 亞洲茄子...450公克 (12兩) |
| 絞肉 (豬、牛或雞)...150公克 (4兩) |

1
- 蔥、薑、蒜末...各2大匙
- 辣椒醬...1小匙

2
- 醬油...4大匙
- 酒、糖...各2小匙
- 高湯或水...4大匙
- 玉米粉...½大匙

飯...2碗

1　茄子去皮，切長條，放入多量水內浸泡備用，使用前瀝乾水份。

2　油3大匙燒熱，炒香1料隨入絞肉炒熟後，放入茄子翻炒數分鐘至軟，再加2料燒開攪拌成濃稠狀，隨意撒上蔥花即可加在飯上與蔬菜配食。

魚香醬 是以1及2料烹調而成。其特色是使用多量的蔥、薑、蒜、辣椒醬等香辛料。魚香醬其實並沒有魚在裡面，而是民間常以此調味方式來烹調魚類而得名。魚香肉絲是另一道著名的四川菜。

EGGPLANT WITH SPICY GARLIC SAUCE OVER RICE

【 SERVES 2 】

| 1 lb. (450g) Asian eggplants |
| ⅓ lb. (150g) ground pork, beef or chicken |

1
- 2 T. ea. (minced): green onion, ginger root, garlic
- 1 t. chili paste

2
- 4 T. soy sauce
- 2 t. ea.: cooking wine, sugar
- 4 T. stock or water
- ½ T. cornstarch

2 c. cooked rice

1　Peel eggplants and cut into long, thick strips. Soak in water then set aside. Drain thoroughly before use.

2　Heat 3T. oil, stir-fry 1 until fragrant. Add meat and stir-fry until cooked. Add eggplant and stir-fry several minutes until soft; add mixture 2 and bring to boil until sauce thickens. Add chopped green onions as desired. Remove and serve with rice and vegetables.

SPICY GARLIC SAUCE is comprised of 1 and 2 sauces. Its unique flavor is derived from combining a large quantity of green onions, ginger, garlic, and chili sauce. In Chinese, "Spicy Garlic Sauce" is literally called "Fragrant Fish Sauce." Actually, the sauce does not contain fish. Its name comes from its frequent accompaniment in a variety of fish dishes. One other famous application of "Fragrant Fish Sauce," or more accurately, "Spicy Garlic Sauce", is "Shredded Pork with Spicy Garlic Sauce".

咖哩雞飯

【 2人份 】

雞肉...225公克 (6兩)

☐1 鹽...¼小匙
酒、玉米粉...各1大匙

☐2 洋蔥丁...½杯
咖哩粉*、麵粉...各3大匙

☐3 馬鈴薯丁、紅蘿蔔丁
...共225公克(6兩)

☐4 鹽...½小匙，糖...½大匙
罐頭雞湯...1 杯，水...2杯

飯...2碗

1 肉切丁，調入☐1料拌均。

2 油4大匙燒熱，依序將☐2料放入炒香，再入☐3料炒拌，隨加☐4料，以大火煮開後改中火煮約20分鐘至馬鈴薯熟軟，燒煮時需隨時攪動以免黏鍋。最後加肉丁煮5分鐘至熟，可隨意加牛奶至喜歡的濃稠度即可澆在飯上食用。

* 咖哩粉的種類很多，味道及辣度各不同，可選擇適合自己的品牌使用。

CURRY CHICKEN OVER RICE

[SERVES 2]

½ lb. (225g) boneless chicken

☐1 ¼ t. salt
1 T. ea.: cooking wine, cornstarch

☐2 ½ c. diced onions
3 T. ea.: flour, curry powder*

☐3 ½ lb (225g) total (diced): potato, carrots.

☐4 ½ t. salt; ½ T. sugar
1 c. canned chicken broth; 2 c. water

2 c. cooked rice

1 Dice chicken and mix with ☐1.

2 Heat 4T. oil, add ☐2 in the order listed, and stir-fry until fragrant. Add ☐3 stir-fry briefly and add ☐4; bring to boil over high heat. Reduce heat to medium and cook 20 minutes, stirring occasionally until potatoes are cooked. Add chicken and cook 5 minutes until cooked through. Milk may be added to get desired consistency. Remove and serve with rice.

* There are many varieties of curry powder, all different in flavor and degree of spiciness. Choose to individual preference.

肉燥飯 SAVORY MEAT SAUCE OVER RICE

【 台灣菜 】	【 4人份 】
絞肉...450公克(12兩)	
油蔥酥...3大匙	
香菇 (泡軟切丁)...2朵	
雞蛋(煮熟、去殼)...6個	
1 五香粉...隨意	
醬油...½杯	
2 酒...2大匙	
糖...1大匙	
水...2½杯	
飯...4碗	

1 油4大匙與油蔥酥放入鍋內略炒，隨入香菇炒香、絞肉炒開至變色，再加雞蛋及1料翻炒至蛋表面上色，再加2料燒開，蓋鍋以小火煮40分鐘即成肉燥，煮時注意火侯以免燒乾。

2 飯盛碗內，隨喜好加肉燥及滷蛋。

■ 台灣路邊攤常見的小吃中，很多都以肉燥來做變化，因肉燥味香濃可口，煮一鍋可用來拌飯、麵、米粉、河粉或加入湯麵，非常方便。

焢肉飯　煮肉燥時加入三層肉一起滷，滷好的三層肉即為焢肉可與飯食用。
滷豆乾　將豆腐乾在肉燥湯汁內燒煮10分鐘入味，可當小菜。
台南米糕　用小碗裝香Q的糯米飯，澆上適量的肉燥及滷汁，搭配少許魚鬆、煮熟花生及香菜即成。
嘉義雞肉飯　飯盛碗內，把煮熟的雞肉撕成絲放在飯上，隨喜好加肉燥及滷汁，再加數片醃漬的黃蘿蔔。

【 TAIWANESE CUISINE 】	【 SERVES 4 】
1 lb. (450g) ground pork	
3 T. fried shallots	
2 Chinese black mushrooms, softened in water and diced	
6 eggs, hard boiled and shelled	
1 five spice powder as desired	
½ c. soy sauce	
2 2 T. cooking wine	
1 T. sugar; 2½ c. water	
4 c. cooked rice	

1 Heat 4 T. oil, sauté shallots lightly and then add mushrooms, stir-fry until fragrant. Add pork, stir-fry until color changes. Add in eggs and 1; stir until eggs are coated with the sauce. Add 2, and bring to boil; cover, turn to low heat and simmer for 40 minutes, watch heat carefully to avoid evaporating all the liquid.

2 Put rice in a bowl. Spoon on the meat sauce and stewed eggs to personal preference.

■ In the ubiquitous food stands that line the streets of Taiwan, "Savory Meat Sauce" is a staple of many delicious dishes. Its flavor, uniquely robust and aromatic, blends marvelously with rice, noodles, rice vermicelli, or fresh rice noodles. Keeping a pot of "Savory Meat Sauce" on hand is very convenient because of its many applications.

MARBLED PORK AND SAVORY MEAT SAUCE OVER RICE Add pieces of marbled pork to cook with the above ground pork. The braised marble pork goes well over rice.
SAVORY PRESSED BEAN CURD Cook pressed bean curd in the "Savory Meat Sauce" for about 10 minutes; when thinly sliced, they make for an excellent appetizer.
TAINAN STICKY RICE Fill small bowl with cooked glutinous rice, top with some "Savory Meat Sauce", sprinkle with ground fried fish, roasted peanuts, and cilantro.
JIA YI CHICKEN OVER RICE Fill bowl with cooked rice, top with shredded cooked chicken. Add "Savory Meat Sauce" and garnish with Japanese pickled radish.

紅燒牛腩飯　BRAISED BEEF OVER RICE

牛腩(切塊)*(見100頁) ...900公克(1½斤)	2 lbs. (900g) beef brisket* (p.100), cut in pieces
1 蒜頭(拍扁)...8瓣 薑...8片 辣椒...1枝	1 8 garlic cloves, smashed 8 ginger root slices 1 chili pepper
2 醬油...½杯，酒...2大匙	2 ½ c. soy sauce 2 T. cooking wine
3 水...8杯，八角...1朶	3 8 c. water 1 star anise
糖...1大匙 4 白蘿蔔塊、紅蘿蔔塊 ...共450公克(12兩)	1 T. sugar 4 1 lb. (450g) total (cut in pieces): white radish, carrots
5 玉米粉、水...各2大匙	5 2 T. ea.: cornstarch, water
飯...4碗	4 c. cooked rice

1　油2大匙燒熱，先將1料炒香再入牛腩略炒，加2料炒拌燒開5分鐘讓牛肉上色，再加3料煮開，蓋鍋以小火燒煮1½小時至肉略熟軟。

2　將4料放入已燒好的牛肉湯內 (湯汁宜滿過材料)，燒開後以中火燒煮約20分鐘至蘿蔔熟透汁略收乾，以5料勾芡即可與飯配食。

＊　可以牛腱(見103頁)取代，牛肉因產地的不同，燒煮的時間也不同，必須略做調整。若湯汁剩太多或太少，皆會影響菜餚的鹹淡。

■　若有現成的香菜莖或蔥段等加4料時一起放入燒煮，可增加菜餚香味。

1　Heat 2 T. oil, stir-fry 1 until fragrant. Add beef and stir lightly. Stir in 2, mix well and boil 5 minutes until meat is brown. Add 3 and bring to boil again. Cover and cook over low heat for 1½ hours or until meat is tender.

2　Add 4 to the beef; beef and vegetables should be covered by liquid, let boil, lower heat to medium and cook 20 minutes or until vegetables are cooked and liquid is almost evaporated. Add in mixture 5 to thicken; serve with rice.

＊　Beef shank (p.103) may be used for beef brisket. Adjust cooking time in recognition of the origin of the beef (range vs. stock yard) to have the proper amount of liquid left. Too much or too little liquid remaining will affect the saltiness of the dish.

■　Pieces of coriander stem or green onions may be added to 4 to enhance the flavor of the dish.

紅燒肉飯

【 4人份 】

腿肉...450公克(12兩)

① 蒜頭(拍破)...4瓣
酒、醬油...各4大匙

② 糖...½大匙
水...1½杯
油豆腐...4塊 (無亦可)
八角...½朵
蔥(切段)...3枝
飯...4碗

1 將肉切塊與①料放入鍋內煮開，
煮滾一分鐘，翻拌見肉均勻上
色，再加②料燒開，蓋鍋以小
火煮30分鐘，煮至湯汁快收乾，
拌入蔥段即可與飯配食。

■ 此道菜選擇略肥的肉來做口感
較佳。起鍋前若開大火將肉汁
燒至快收乾，則肉本身的味道
較濃；但一般家庭在做這道菜
時會多留些肉汁，以肉汁拌飯，
是不錯的吃法。

BRAISED PORK IN SOY SAUCE OVER RICE

[SERVES 4]

1 lb. (450g) pork shoulder or fresh bacon

① 4 garlic cloves, smashed
4 T. ea.: cooking wine, soy sauce

② ½ T. sugar
1½ c. water
4 deep-fried tofu pieces (optional)
½ star anise
3 green onions, cut into pieces
4 c. cooked rice

■ This dish is most appetizing when cooked with marbled meat. If preferred, turn heat to high after simmering to reduce the meat juices, thus increasing the robust flavor to the meat. Many households prefer having some meat juices to accentuate the rice; its texture and flavor of rice is significantly enhanced.

1 Cut meat into 1"x1½" (2.5 x 4 cm) pieces. Bring ① and the meat to boil and cook for 1 minute; mix well until meat is browned evenly. Add ② and bring to boil again, cover and cook over low heat for 30 minutes. When the liquid is almost evaporated, sprinkle with green onions. Remove and serve with rice.

紅燒豬蹄飯

[4人份]

前腿蹄...1200公克(2斤)	
醬油...1½大匙	
蔥段 ...6段	
蒜頭(拍破)...4瓣	
1	水...3杯，醬油...¾杯
	酒...1大匙，冰糖或糖...1大匙
	八角...1朵 或五香粉...¼小匙
飯...4碗	

1　豬蹄剁成5-6塊，入滾水中川燙撈出，瀝乾水份，抹上醬油備用。

2　油4大匙燒熱，把蔥、蒜炒香，將豬蹄外皮煎炒至金黃色後，加1料以中火燒煮40分鐘，至肉汁剩一半，用筷子插入試試是否已軟，即可離火與飯配食。

■ 相傳吃豬蹄可以去霉運並帶來福氣。加八角可增加香味。豬蹄含有膠質，煮的時間足夠時才會軟Q入味。

BRAISED PIG'S FEET OVER RICE

[SERVES 4]

2⅔ lbs. (1200g) pig's forefeet	
1½ T. soy sauce	
6 pieces green onion	
4 garlic cloves, smashed	
1	3 c. water; ¾ c. soy sauce; 1 T. cooking wine
	1 T. rock sugar or sugar
	1 star anise or ¼ t. five spice powder
4 c. cooked rice	

1　Chop pig's feet into 5 or 6 pieces; blanch in boiling water. Remove and drain. Spoon soy sauce over surface of pig's feet, set aside.

2　Heat 4 T. oil, stir-fry green onions and garlic until fragrant. Put in pig's feet and fry until surface is golden brown. Add 1 and cook over medium heat for 40 minutes. Cook until liquid is reduced to half and a chopstick can penetrate the meat easily. Remove from heat and serve with rice.

■ The Chinese associate the consumption of pig's feet with the power to ward off bad luck and bring good fortune. Rock sugar brings out the luster of braised meat; star anise adds to the aroma. Pig's feet contain gelatin which requires sufficient simmering time to soften and to acquire a chewy consistency.

麻婆豆腐飯　　MA-PO TOFU OVER RICE

麻婆豆腐飯

【 四川菜 】	【 2人份 】	【 SZECHWAN CUISINE 】	【 SERVES 2 】

嫩豆腐*...300公克(8兩)　　　　⅔ lb (300g) tofu*, soft

① 蒜末、薑末...各1小匙　　　　① 1 t. ea. (minced): garlic, ginger root

蔥末...1大匙　　　　1 T. chopped green onion

絞肉(牛或豬)... 150公克(4兩)　　　⅓ lb. (150g) ground beef or pork

辣豆瓣醬、酒...各1大匙　　　1 T. ea.: chili bean paste, cooking wine

醬油...2大匙　　　　2 T. soy sauce

② 水...1½杯　　　　② 1½ c. water

鹽...⅓小匙　　　　⅓ t. salt

③ 玉米粉...1½大匙　　　　③ 1½ T. cornstarch

水...1大匙　　　　1 T. water

④ 蒜苗絲、青豆或蔥花...2大匙　　　④ 2 T. shredded fresh garlic or chopped green onion

花椒粉(若無亦可)...¼小匙　　　¼ t. Szechwan pepper powder (optional)

飯...2碗　　　　2 c. cooked rice

1　豆腐切丁或切薄片。

2　油3大匙燒熱，將①料依序放入炒開至肉變色，再入②料及豆腐燒開，隨即改中火煮3分鐘，以③料勾芡，並撒上④料即可澆在飯上食用。

＊　若用普通豆腐則將②料內的水改為1¾杯。

■　麻婆豆腐雖然材料及做法簡單，卻是四川名菜之一。它的故事由來也很有趣，據說過去有位麻臉的阿婆與其夫經營飯舖，麻婆就近利用手邊的辣椒、豆瓣醬、青蒜、花椒和肉末，燒出一道麻辣鮮香的豆腐，沒想到可口美味而流傳千古，而麻婆豆腐之名就不逕而走。

1　Cut tofu into small cubes or slices.

2　Heat 3 T. oil, add ① in the order listed and stir-fry until meat changes color. Add ② and tofu, bring to boil; turn heat to medium and cook for 3 minutes. Add mixture ③ and stir to thicken. Sprinkle with ④. Pour over rice and serve.

＊　If regular tofu is used, increase the water in ② to 1¾ c.

■　Since the ingredients in Ma-Po Tofu are quite common and its method of preparation simple, it is one of the most famous Szechwan dishes. It has an interesting story as well. Legend has it that a pock-faced ("Ma") old wife ("Po") ran a restaurant with her husband. She combined whatever ingredients were in her kitchen: chilies, hot bean paste, garlic, Szechwan pepper, and ground pork. The outcome was a fantastically tasty dish, named for its creator that has enjoyed an enduring reputation.

獅子頭飯

【 2人份 】

絞肉(牛、雞或豬)...225公克(6兩)

1
蛋...1個
豆腐(壓碎)...⅓杯或水...2大匙
鹽、麻油...各⅓小匙
胡椒...少許，玉米粉...1½大匙

蔥、薑末...各1小匙

2
醬油、酒...各1大匙
水...½杯，蠔油...½大匙
糖...1小匙

3 水...1大匙，玉米粉...½大匙

飯...2碗

1 絞肉加 1 料仔細攪勻再拌入蔥薑，做成6個肉餅。

2 油1大匙燒熱，將肉餅放入鍋內，兩面各煎至金黃色，加 2 料燒開再以 3 料勾芡即可與飯及蔬菜配食。

■ 絞肉內加入豆腐或水，主要是使肉滑嫩。傳統獅子頭的作法是將拌好的絞肉做成肉丸子後煎炸再紅燒，由於狀似獅子頭，因而得名。此處將肉丸子略壓扁是因為較易煎熟，可縮短烹調時間。

LION'S HEAD ON RICE

[SERVES 2]

½ lb. (225g) ground beef, chicken, or pork

1
1 egg
⅓ c. mashed tofu or 2 T. water
⅓ t. ea.: salt, sesame oil
dash of pepper
1½ T. cornstarch

1 t. ea.: minced green onion, ginger root

2
1 T. ea.: soy sauce, cooking wine
½ c. water; 1 t. sugar
½ T. oyster sauce or soy sauce

3 1 T. water; ½ T. cornstarch

2 c. cooked rice

1 Mix 1 well with ground meat, and add green onion and ginger. Form mixture into 6 meatballs and flatten slightly.

2 Heat 1 T. oil and fry meat patties until both sides are golden brown. Add 2 and bring to boil. Add mixture 3 to thicken. Serve with rice and vegetables.

■ To soften the meat, mix ground pork with soft tofu or water. The traditional way to prepare Lion's Head (large pan-fried meatballs) is to make large meatballs out of ground pork mixed with seasoning. Slightly flatten meatballs to shorten pan-frying time, and then braise in reduced soy sauce. The dish is called "Lion's Head" because the shape of the meat patties resembles a lion's head.

豉汁烤魚飯

[廣東菜]

[4人份]

魚排肉...600公克(1斤)	

1 料:
- 醬油、酒...各2大匙
- 糖...1小匙
- 豆豉...2大匙
- 薑、蒜末...各1大匙
- 蔥末...2大匙
- 辣椒末...1大匙
- 罐頭雞湯...¼杯

飯...4碗

1 魚排整片或切4片。烤盤鋪鋁紙並塗上2大匙油，放入魚，淋上[1]料後包好備用。

2 預熱烤箱至200℃ (400°F)，放入魚烤20分鐘至用筷子可輕易插入後取出連汁與飯及青菜配食。

豉汁 是以豆豉為主加入剁碎的蔥薑蒜來提味，是廣東菜裡常用的烹調手法，蒸或炒皆適宜，除魚外還可應用在其他海鮮、雞、排骨、豆腐或蔬菜等。知名的菜餚有豉椒牛肉、豉汁蛤蜊等。

BAKED FISH WITH BLACK BEAN SAUCE ON RICE

[CANTONESE CUISINE]

[SERVES 4]

- 1⅓ lbs. (600g) salmon fillet

1
- 2 T. ea.: soy sauce, cooking wine
- 1 t. sugar
- 2 T. fermented black beans
- 1 T. ea. (minced): ginger root, garlic
- 2 T. minced green onion
- 1 T. minced chili pepper
- ¼ c. canned chicken broth

- 4 c. cooked rice

1 Use whole fillet, or cut in four pieces. Line a baking pan with aluminum foil and grease the foil with 2 T. oil. Put in the salmon. Pour on ⬜1 then wrap fish with the aluminum foil.

2 Pre-heat oven to 400°F (200°C). Bake fish for 20 minutes or until done. Remove from foil and serve with rice and vegetables.

BLACK BEAN SAUCE is composed of black beans, minced garlic, green onions, and ginger. Commonly used in Cantonese cuisine, this versatile sauce enhances steamed or stir-fried fish, other seafood, chicken, spare-ribs, tofu, or vegetables. Two famous examples include "Beef with Spicy Black Bean Sauce" and "Clams with Black Bean Sauce".

海鮮焗飯 | BAKED SEAFOOD RICE

【 廣東菜 】 【 4人份 】

熟蛤蜊肉*、蝦仁、魚肉
...共450公克 (12兩)

① 紅蘿蔔、青花菜、菠菜
...共450公克(12兩)

奶油(或其他食油)...5大匙

蔥...8段

麵粉...6大匙

② 蛤蜊湯汁*...5杯

酒...1大匙，鹽...1½小匙

糖、胡椒...各¼小匙

起司絲或椰蓉...⅓杯

飯...4碗

1 將①料內的紅蘿蔔切片、青花菜切小
朵；菠菜切段在滾水中川燙撈出，
沖冷水擠乾。

2 奶油略燒熱，先炒蔥段，續加入麵
粉炒拌，再入①、②料攪拌燒開成糊
狀，最後再入海鮮燒滾即成海鮮濃
汁。

3 將飯分別置於4個耐烤的容器內，把
海鮮濃汁澆在飯上，上撒起司粉，
入烤箱以230℃(450℉)烤20分鐘，
至表面呈金黃色。

* 將新鮮蛤蜊洗淨放入滾水內(水宜蓋
滿蛤蜊)，見蛤蜊殼一開即撈出，取
出蛤蜊肉即為熟蛤蜊肉。煮過蛤蜊
的湯汁濾去砂質再加水成5杯，即為
蛤蜊湯汁。

■ 燙煮海鮮時不宜煮太久，肉熟即
可；喜歡奶味者，在海鮮濃汁起鍋
前加入濃縮奶水。

[CANTONESE CUISINE] [SERVES 4]

1 lb (450g) total: cooked clam meat*, shelled shrimp, fish fillets

① 1 lb (450g) total: carrots, broccoli, spinach

5 T. butter or cooking oil

8 pieces green onion

6 T. flour

② 5 c. liquid reserved from cooking clams

1 T. cooking wine

1½ t. salt

¼ t. ea.: sugar, pepper

⅓ c. shredded Mozzarella or coconut

4 c. cooked rice

1 From ①, slice carrots and cut broccoli into pieces; cut spinach into 1½" (4 cm) pieces. Blanch spinach in boiling water, rinse in cold water immediately, lightly squeeze out water. Set aside.

2 Heat butter, stir-fry onions, add flour and continue to stir-fry. Add in ① and ②; stir mixture and boil to thicken. Add the seafood; bring to a boil to make seafood sauce.

3 Preheat oven to 450°F (230°C). Divide rice into four ramekins; pour seafood mixture on the rice. Sprinkle mozzarella on top and bake for 20 minutes or until surface turns golden brown.

* Scrub and wash clams. Immerse clams in boiling water, cook until clams open and immediately remove from boiling water. Strain liquid through a sieve to remove any sand and reserve 5 c. for ②. Remove meat from shells.

■ Seafood can easily overcook, they should be removed as soon as they are done. If a creamy taste is preferred, mix in evaporated milk or whipping cream to the seafood sauce before baking.

【 上海菜 】

【 4人份 】

雞腿肉...450公克(12兩)

青江菜...450公克(12兩)

1
蔥白...6段，薑...6片

香菇(切絲)...4朵

2
罐頭雞湯...1¾杯

鹽....¾小匙，胡椒...¼小匙

醬油...1小匙，米...2杯

1 雞腿肉拭乾水份切塊，青江菜略切。

2 油1大匙燒熱，把雞肉煎成金黃色後取出。

3 油1大匙燒熱，先炒香**1**料再入青江菜及2大匙的水，蓋鍋見水蒸汽冒出即盛出。

4 把**2**料、雞肉、及炒熟的青江菜等放入電鍋內，蒸熟即成雞肉菜飯。

■ 一般煮飯米與水的比例為1：1，但煮菜飯時，因蔬菜中也含水份，故將雞湯減量為1¾杯。

上海菜飯 炒好的青江菜與**2**料煮成的菜飯。通常與煎排骨、炸排骨(見67頁)或廣式臘腸配食。

STEAMED CHICKEN RICE WITH GREENS

【 SHANGHAI CUISINE 】

【 SERVES 4 】

1 lb. (450g) boneless chicken legs

1 lb. (450g) bok choy

1
6 ea.: white part of green onion pieces, ginger root slices

4 Chinese black mushrooms, softened in water and shredded

2
1¾ c. canned chicken broth; ¾ t. salt

¼ t. pepper; 1 t. soy sauce; 2 c. rice

1 Wash and pat dry chicken legs, then cut into pieces. Cut bok choy into pieces.

2 Heat 1T. oil, pan-fry chicken until it is golden brown.

3 Heat 1 T. oil, stir-fry **1** until fragrant. Add bok choy and 2 T. water. Cover and cook until steam appears; remove.

4 Place chicken, bok choy and **2** in a rice cooker; cook until rice is done.

■ Standard ratio for rice and water is 1:1 for cooking rice. When cooking rice with vegetables as in this recipe, reduce chicken broth from 2 cups to 1¾ cups due to the water contained in the vegetables.

SHANGHAI RICE WITH GREENS
Steam rice with bok choy and **2** to make this popular Shanghai style dish. Serve with pan-fried pork chops or deep-fried pork chops (p.67) for a balanced diet.

海南雞飯

【 4人份 】

全雞...900公克(1½斤)

① 蔥白...4支，薑...4片

② 鹽、酒...各2小匙

米...2杯，蒜頭(拍破)...2瓣

③ 薑末...2大匙，蔥末...1大匙

鹽...½小匙

1　將①料拍扁與②料抓拌後抹擦雞的表面，醃2小時後置於蒸盤，米洗淨瀝乾。

2　多量水燒開，將醃過的雞以大火蒸35分鐘至熟，取出待雞降至常溫後剁塊，蒸雞的餘汁留1大匙備用，剩餘雞汁加水成2杯，與米及蒜放入電鍋內煮成飯。

3　油1大匙燒熱，淋入③料內，再拌1大匙雞汁即為沾料。

4　煮成的飯可搭配番茄或黃瓜，雞塊沾沾料食用，也可以沾醬油。

■　此道菜在南洋一帶很盛行，在廣式餐廳中也很普遍，若蒸雞不方便，可改用水煮，利用煮雞的雞湯煮飯。

HAINAN CHICKEN RICE

[SERVES 4]

2 lbs. (900g) chicken

① 4 white part of green onion pieces; 4 slices ginger root

② 2 t. ea.: salt, cooking wine

2 c. rice

2 garlic cloves, smashed

③ 2 T. minced ginger root; 1 T. minced green onion; ½ t. salt

1　Smash ① then mix with ②. Rub on chicken inside and out, and marinate chicken for 2 hours then place on a plate to steam later. Rinse and drain rice.

2　Boil a generous amount of water over high heat; steam chicken for 35 minutes or until cooked through. Remove and let cool to room temperature, then cut into pieces and set aside. Reserve 1 T. of the residual liquid to make sauce. Add water to the remaining liquid to produce 2 c. Add rice and garlic, cook in the rice cooker until done.

3　Place ③ in a small bowl. Heat 1 T. oil and pour over ③; mix with the reserved 1 T. of chicken liquid to make a dipping sauce.

4　Cooked rice can be served with tomatoes or cucumbers. Dipping sauce or soy sauce may be used to dip chicken.

■　This dish enjoys immense popularity in Southeast Asia, and is commonly served in Cantonese restaurants. If it is not convenient to steam the chicken, poaching works just as well. The resultant chicken broth may be used to cook the rice.

油飯 TAIWANESE STICKY RICE

【 台灣菜 】 【 4人份 】

長糯米...2杯

① 水...1⅓杯
油...1大匙

② 油蔥酥...3大匙
蝦米...2大匙
香菇(泡軟切絲)...5朵

瘦豬肉絲*...225公克(6兩)

③ 酒...1大匙
麻油...1大匙
醬油...3大匙
糖、鹽、胡椒...各¼小匙

1 糯米洗淨加①料放入電鍋煮成糯米飯。

2 油4大匙略燒熱,將②料依序放入炒香,隨即放入豬肉炒開變色,再加③料炒勻,趁熱拌入煮好的糯米飯即成油飯。

* 肉的份量可減少,加入1條切小丁的台式香腸或乾魷魚絲,可做出另一種風味的油飯。

■ 油飯在習俗上為七夕祭拜兒童守護神七娘媽的供品,因而在慶祝滿月時,多以油飯當作分贈親友的賀禮。

【 TAIWANESE CUISINE 】 【 SERVES 4 】

2 c. long grain glutinous rice

① 1⅓ c. water
1 T. oil

② 3 T. fried shallots
2 T. dried shrimp
5 Chinese black mushrooms, softened in water and shredded

½ lb. (225g) shredded lean pork*

③ 1 T. ea.: cooking wine, sesame oil
3 T. soy sauce
¼ t. ea.: sugar, salt, pepper

1 Wash and drain rice; add ①, place in rice cooker and cook until done.

2 Heat 4T. oil, add in ② in the order listed; stir until fragrant. Add pork, stir-fry until meat is separated and color changes. Add ③; mix well. Immediately mix with cooked rice.

* For variation, reduce the amount of pork and add diced Taiwanese sausage or dried shredded squid.

■ Taiwanese Sticky Rice is traditionally served as an offering to the Mother of Seven Maidens, the Protector Goddess of Children during commemoration ceremonies. It is served as part of a meal and sent as a thank-you gift to family and friends who are invited to the one-month birthday celebration of babies.

紅蟳米糕 活蟹一隻放入滾水內川燙並打開蟹殼,除去腮及胃袋,把表面刷洗淨後,切塊拌少許鹽、薑、酒,置於做好的油飯上再蒸15分鐘,至蟹肉熟。香味四溢的蟹黃汁淋在油飯上,令人垂涎三尺,這是台灣喜慶宴客席中的傳統大菜。

鹹飯 用一般的取代糯米,其他材料及作法同上。

STEAMED CRAB ON STICKY RICE Blanch the live crab in boiling water. Detach the body from its shell and remove the lung pieces and stomach. Clean the shell and the carcass by brushing them before cutting the body into pieces. Mix the crab pieces with salt, ginger, and cooking wine, and place on the cooked sticky rice. Continue steaming for 15 minutes until the crab is cooked. The fragrant crab broth drizzled over steamed sticky rice is a famous mainstay of traditional Taiwanese banquets.

TAIWANESE SAVORY RICE Substitute ordinary rice for glutinous rice; other ingredients and methods remain the same.

臘味煲飯

【 廣東菜 】

【 4人份 】

廣式臘腸、臘肉*(圖1)
...共300公克(8兩)
米...2杯
醬油...1½大匙

1 臘腸及臘肉洗淨,臘肉去皮。

2 米洗淨加2杯水放砂鍋內以大火燒開,將米略攪一下放入臘腸及臘肉再蓋鍋以小火燜煮8分鐘,熄火再燜10分鐘,將臘腸及臘肉取出切片備用。

3 把鍋底的一層鍋巴輕輕翻拌,上置臘腸及臘肉後澆上醬油,與炒熟或燙熟的青菜配食。

* 臘腸、臘肉是將豬肉加入醃料再處理後,晾乾製成,超市有售。通常蒸、烤或煎後即可與飯配食。

■ 煲飯是廣東菜普遍的簡餐之一,煮飯時把肉等材料放入與米一起煮熟,澆在飯上的醬油可採用濃稠狀的醬油露,喜食辣者可加些新鮮辣椒。

CANTONESE CLAY POT SAUSAGE AND RICE

【 CANTONESE CUISINE 】

【 SERVES 4 】

⅔ lb. (300g) Cantonese sausage, salted pork* (Fig. 1)
2 c. rice; 1½ T. soy sauce

1

1 Rinse sausage and salted pork and drain. Remove salted pork skin.

2 Rinse rice until water runs clear; put in a clay pot and add 2 c. water and cook over high heat until boiling, stirring lightly. Arrange sausage and pork on top of rice; cover and simmer over low heat for 8 minutes. Turn off heat and let stand for 10 minutes. Remove sausage and pork; slice thinly and set aside.

3 Using a spatula or large spoon, bring crisp rice from bottom of pot to the top and mix lightly. Arrange sausage and pork slices on top of the rice. Pour on soy sauce and serve with cooked vegetables.

* Cantonese sausage and salted pork are marinated and air-dried. Available in most Chinese markets, these sausages and salted pork may be steamed, baked, or pan-fried to accompany steamed rice.

■ Clay pot rice is a common one-dish meal in Cantonese cuisine. To prepare, cook meat, rice, and other ingredients together. Drizzle with soy sauce or soy paste and serve. If preferred, add fresh chili pepper.

炸排骨飯

【 2人份 】

大排骨肉2片...450公克(12兩)

① 醬油...2大匙，五香粉...⅛小匙
蒜末...½大匙，糖...1大匙
胡椒...⅛小匙，蛋黃...1個

蕃薯粉或玉米粉...½杯

燙熟青菜...適量

飯...2碗

1　大排骨肉搥鬆後，加入①料拌勻醃10分鐘後，再沾滿蕃薯粉備炸。

2　炸油燒熱，放入排骨炸至表面略凝固，改以中火炸至肉熟表面酥脆撈出，切塊排在飯上，旁邊擺燙熟青菜。

■　酸菜是排骨飯的好搭檔，調理簡便，只需將酸菜切碎加少許辣椒、鹽與糖同炒即可。炸好的排骨肉可沾椒鹽、番茄醬、醬油等食用。

炸雞腿飯　改以炸好的雞腿(見95頁)排在飯上，旁邊擺燙熟青菜即可。

FRIED PORK CHOPS WITH RICE

[SERVES 2]

2 large pork chops, 1 lb. (450g)

① 2 T. soy sauce; ⅛ t. five spice powder
½ T. minced garlic
1 T. sugar; ⅛ t. pepper
1 egg yolk

½ c. potato starch or cornstarch

cooked vegetables, as desired

2 c. cooked rice

1　Pound the pork chops until tender. Marinate with ① for 10 minutes; then dredge in cornstarch and set aside.

2　Heat enough oil to deep-fry pork chops, and fry until surface is firm. Turn heat to medium, continue to fry until golden brown and meat is cooked. Remove and cut into pieces and place on rice. Serve with cooked vegetables.

■　Pickled mustard cabbage is an excellent accompaniment to fried pork chops and is easy to prepare. To prepare, chop the pickled mustard cabbage then stir-fry with a pinch of salt, sugar, and chili pepper. Pork chop may be served with pepper salt, ketchup, or soy sauce.

CRISPY CHICKEN LEGS WITH RICE
Place fried chicken legs (see p.95) on rice and garnish with blanched vegetables.

醬油蛋酥炒飯

【 2人份 】

蛋...3個

蒜末...1大匙

1　醬油... 1½大匙

　　鹽、胡椒...各⅛小匙

　　麻油... 1小匙

飯...2碗

1　蛋打散成蛋液。

2　油4大匙燒熱，炒香蒜末，將蛋液倒入鍋內，以大火炒至焦黃色有香味成蛋酥，續入①料拌勻，再入飯拌炒均勻，盛起即可。

■　此為台灣家常炒飯，特點是將蛋炒至香酥。

TAIWANESE FRIED RICE

【 SERVES 2 】

3 eggs

1 T. minced garlic

1 **1½ T. soy sauce**

　⅛ t. ea.: salt, pepper

　1 t. sesame oil

2 c. cooked rice

1　Beat eggs and set aside.

2　Heat 4 T. oil, stir-fry garlic until fragrant, add eggs and stir-fry over high heat until crispy and color turns dark brown. Add ① and mix well; add rice and continue to stir-fry to mix well. Serve.

■　The uniqueness of this popular Taiwanese style fried rice is to fry the eggs until dark brown and crispy.

咖哩炒飯

【 2人份 】

絞肉...150公克 (4兩)
洋蔥丁...⅓杯
① 咖哩粉...½大匙
糖、鹽...各½小匙
② 青椒丁、熟紅蘿蔔丁...共1杯
飯...2碗

1 油3大匙燒熱，炒香洋蔥後並將肉炒開至變色，入①料翻炒後，隨入②料與飯拌炒均勻即可。

肉絲炒飯 以肉絲替代絞肉，不加咖哩粉，其他材料及作法不變即為簡易的肉絲炒飯。

CURRY FRIED RICE

【 SERVES 2 】

⅓ lb. (150g) ground pork
⅓ c. diced onions
① ½ T. curry powder
½ t. ea.: sugar, salt
② 1 c. total (diced): green bell pepper and cooked carrot
2 c. cooked rice

1 Heat 3 T. oil, stir-fry onions until fragrant; add meat and stir to separate, fry until color changes. Add ①, mix well; add ② and rice. Continue to stir-fry until mixed well. Serve.

EASY FRIED RICE Replace ground pork with shredded meat and omit curry powder. All the other ingredients and procedures are the same as above. This is the simplest and most popular fried rice dish. Adding other ingredients to this basic dish can create a variety of tasty fried rice treats.

蛋包飯

【 2人份 】

1 ⌈ 蛋...4個，鹽...⅛小匙
  ⌊ 洋蔥丁...¼杯
    絞肉或肉絲...150公克 (4兩)

2 ⌈ 番茄醬...2大匙，糖...1小匙
  ⌊ 鹽、胡椒...各¼小匙，飯...2碗

1 將1料打散成蛋液。

2 油3大匙燒熱，炒香洋蔥後並
  將肉炒開至變色，入2料拌炒
  均勻即為番茄醬炒飯，盛起分
  成二份。

3 鍋燒熱，以紙巾沾油塗抹鍋
  面，將一半的蛋液倒入煎成圓
  形蛋皮，轉中火將蛋皮煎半熟
  時，將事先炒好的一份炒飯放
  入蛋皮中，把兩邊合起續煎至
  蛋熟，盛入盤中，同樣的做法
  另做一份，淋上番茄醬即可食
  用。

■ 煎蛋皮時，油溫太低或鍋中的
  油太多時會導致蛋易滑動難
  煎，所以鍋燒熱後用廚房紙巾
  沾油塗抹鍋子上，蛋液放入後
  即與鍋面輕貼，一轉動即成圓
  形。

FRIED RICE OMELET

[SERVES 2]

1 ⌈ 4 eggs; ⅛ t. salt
  ⌊ ¼ c. diced onions
    ⅓ lb. (150g) ground pork or shredded pork

2 ⌈ 2 T. ketchup
  │ 1 t. sugar
  │ ¼ t. ea.: salt, pepper
  ⌊ 2 c. cooked rice

1 Beat 1 well and set aside.

2 Heat 3 T. oil and stir-fry onions until fragrant. Add meat and stir-fry to separate and change color. Add 2 and stir-fry to mix well; divide into two portions and set aside.

3 Heat a wok over high heat and wipe with an oiled paper towel. Pour ½ of the beaten eggs into the wok; flatten to form a large thin "pancake" by rotating the wok. Turn heat to medium and fry until eggs are partially cooked. Place one portion of the rice in the center of the "pancake" and fold over; fry until omelet is completely cooked. Remove and put on a serving plate. Repeat process for the second omelet. Serve with ketchup.

■ Heat the pan and brush on cooking oil with a paper kitchen towel. If the pan is over low heat or if there is excessive oil, the egg will slide and cook unevenly. Pour beaten egg in the pan and gently rock the pan; the egg will spread to form a circle.

番茄蛋炒飯

蛋(打散)...3個

洋蔥丁...⅓杯

1
- 糖、鹽...各½小匙
- 胡椒...⅛小匙
- 麻油...1小匙

2
- 飯...2碗
- 番茄丁...½杯
- 蔥花...¼杯

1　油2大匙燒熱，以大火將蛋液炒成金黃色剛熟即盛起備用。

2　鍋內再加1大匙油燒熱，炒香洋蔥後，與1料翻炒，隨入2料與蛋拌炒均勻即可。

揚州炒飯 炒飯內不加番茄即為一般的蛋炒飯，蛋炒飯內加入豐富的佐料如切丁的海參、叉燒及蝦仁，並隨喜好變化加雞丁、青豆、紅蘿蔔丁等其他材料一起拌炒即成揚州炒飯。其實揚州炒飯就是蛋炒飯的精緻版。

TOMATO FRIED RICE

3 beaten eggs

⅓ c. diced onions

1
- ½ t. ea.: sugar, salt
- ⅛ t. pepper
- 1 t. sesame oil

2
- 2 c. cooked rice
- ½ c. diced tomato
- ¼ c. chopped green onions

1　Heat 2 T. oil, scramble eggs over high heat until slightly solidified and golden in color. Remove and set aside.

2　Heat 1 T. oil, stir-fry onions until fragrant; add 1 and mix well. Add 2 and eggs, stir-fry to mix well. Serve.

YANG CHOW FRIED RICE Fried rice without tomatoes is the common fried rice. What makes ordinary fried rice into extravagant Yang-Chow Fried Rice is the additional ingredients such as green peas, diced sea cucumber, shrimp, Cantonese BBQ Pork, chicken and carrots.

翡翠鴛鴦炒飯

【 2人份 】

蛋(打散)...2個，火腿丁或叉燒肉丁(見145頁)...½杯
香菇丁...2大匙(無亦可)
1 [鹽...⅛小匙，白胡椒粉...⅛小匙
飯...2碗，青江菜...75公克(2兩)，番茄醬...1大匙

1 青江菜放入滾水內燙熟撈出，放入冷水內漂涼，擠乾水份切碎備用。

2 油1大匙燒熱，以大火將蛋液炒成金黃色剛熟即盛起。

3 油2匙燒熱，先入火腿再入香菇炒香，續入飯、蛋及1料拌炒均勻，取出一半炒飯。

4 鍋內剩餘炒飯與青江菜拌炒則為翡翠炒飯；另一半炒飯加入番茄醬炒勻，即成番茄火腿蛋炒飯。二者裝在一盤即鴛鴦炒飯。

■ 雙色炒飯適合做家庭聚會時的餐點，可選擇咖哩粉、醬油、紅椒粉做顏色上的變化。亦可加入青豆及蝦仁成為更豪華的炒飯。

EMERALD FRIED RICE DUET

[SERVES 2]

2 beaten eggs
½ c. diced ham or Cantonese BBQ Pork (p.145)
2 T. diced Chinese black mushrooms
or mushrooms (optional)
1 [**⅛ t. salt; ⅛ t. white pepper**
2 c. cooked rice
2⅔ oz. (75g) bok choy; 1 T. ketchup

1 Blanch bok choy in boiling water; remove and quickly immerse in cold water. Remove and lightly squeeze out water; chop bok choy finely.

2 Heat 1 T. oil, scramble eggs over high heat until slightly solidified and golden in color; remove and set aside.

3 Heat 2 T. oil, stir-fry ham briefly, add mushrooms, cook until fragrant. Add rice, eggs and 1, stir-fry to mix well. Remove ½ portion and set aside.

4 Mix bok choy into the remaining ½ portion in the wok. Mix well and remove. Return the initial ½ portion back in the wok, add ketchup, stir-frying to mix well. Place both portions in a serving dish, making sure to keep colors separate.

■ Two-colored fried rice is highly suitable for the family get-together. Choose from curry powder, soy sauce, or paprika to add color variety to the rice. Green peas and diced shrimp are additions to make the dish even more special.

鮭魚炒飯

[2人份]

1 [
鮭魚肉...150公克 (4兩)，鹽...⅓小匙，蛋(打散)...2個

胡椒或七味粉...¼小匙，飯...2碗

蔥花...¼杯
]

1 將鮭魚以鹽醃10分鐘。

2 油1大匙燒熱，以大火將蛋液炒成金黃色剛熟即盛起備用。

3 油1大匙燒熱，入魚肉煎熟後再鏟鬆，若有魚皮切小塊後放回鍋內，隨入1料與炒好的蛋翻炒均勻，撒上蔥花即可。

■ 前餐剩餘的煎鮭魚或烤鮭魚都可用來做鮭魚炒飯。鮭魚以鹽醃夠味時，炒飯時即不用再加鹽，因鮭魚油脂較多，以魚油來炒飯非常美味可口且香味撲鼻。

鹹魚雞粒炒飯 與鮭魚炒飯類似，唯以鹹魚與雞丁取代鮭魚，味道特殊，是廣式有名的炒飯。

SALMON FRIED RICE

[SERVES 2]

1 [
⅓ lb. (150g) salmon

⅓ t. salt

2 beaten eggs

¼ t. pepper or seven-flavor seasoning

2 c. cooked rice

¼ c. chopped green onions
]

1 Marinate salmon with ⅓ t. salt for 10 minutes.

2 Heat 1 T. oil over high heat and stir-fry eggs until firm and just golden. Remove and set aside.

3 Heat 1 T. oil over high heat and fry salmon until cooked. Cut and separate salmon meat into small pieces. If there is salmon skin, chop it into small pieces; include with remaining salmon. Add 1, and eggs; stir to mix well. Sprinkle with onions and serve.

■ Salmon Fried Rice usually uses leftover baked or pan-fried salmon. If the salmon is salted prior to cooking, there is no need to add salt to the fried rice. Since salmon is a relatively fatty fish, the resultant fried rice is extra fragrant and delicious.

SALTED FISH WITH CHICKEN FRIED RICE Similar to Salmon Fried Rice, salted fish and diced chicken are substituted for salmon. This unique-flavored fried rice is a Cantonese specialty.

鳳梨蝦仁炒飯

蝦仁...150公克(4兩)

1 [蒜末、辣椒末...共1½大匙
叉燒肉(或火腿)丁、青豆...共½杯

2 [魚露*...1½大匙
胡椒粉...⅛小匙

飯...2碗

3 [新鮮或罐頭鳳梨丁...½杯
蔥花...¼杯

1　蝦仁洗淨瀝乾，入熱油鍋內炒熟至變色盛起。

2　將2大匙油燒熱，先炒香1料再加叉燒肉丁、青豆及2料略炒，入飯炒鬆後再加3料與炒熟的蝦仁拌炒均勻，即可盛在盤上。

＊　魚露味鹹，用途與醬油相同，但顏色較醬油淡。

PINEAPPLE SHRIMP FRIED RICE

⅓ lb. (150g) shelled shrimp

1 [1½ T. total (minced): garlic, chili pepper
½ c. total: green peas, diced Cantonese BBQ pork or ham

2 [1½ T fish sauce*
⅛ t. pepper

2 c. cooked rice

3 [½ c. fresh or canned pineapple, diced
¼ c. chopped green onion

1　Rinse shrimp and drain. Heat 1 T. oil, stir-fry shrimp until color changes. Remove and set aside.

2　Heat 2 T oil, stir-fry 1 until fragrant. Add meat, peas and 2, briefly stir-fry; add rice, stir-fry to separate. Add 3 when rice is separated. Return shrimp and mix well. Serve.

＊　Fish sauce is lighter in color but saltier than soy sauce. If fish sauce is not available, soy sauce may be used.

皮蛋瘦肉粥

【 4人份 】

絞肉(豬或雞)...225公克(6兩)

1 ┌ 酒...1小匙
  └ 玉米粉...1大匙

米...1杯

2 ┌ 罐頭雞湯...2杯
  └ 水...10杯

3 ┌ 皮蛋(見142頁)...6個
  │ 鹽...¾小匙
  └ 胡椒... 隨意

4 ┌ 蔥花或芹菜末...4大匙

1 絞肉拌入1料攪拌成泥，皮蛋切丁。

2 米洗淨加2料，燒開後改小火煮40分鐘至米粒軟爛(參考79頁註解)，中途需攪拌以免黏鍋，先取出少許粥加入肉泥攪開後倒回鍋內攪散再燒滾，續入3料再燒開即熄火，撒上4料即可。

THOUSAND-YEAR-OLD EGGS WITH PORK CONGEE
[CANTONESE CUISINE]

[SERVES 4]

½ lb. (225g) ground pork or beef

1 ┌ 1 t. cooking wine
  └ 1 T. cornstarch

1 c. long grain rice

2 ┌ 2 c. canned chicken broth
  └ 10 c. water

3 ┌ 6 preserved eggs (p.142)
  │ ¾ t. salt
  └ dash of pepper

4 ┌ 4 T. chopped green onions or celery

1 Mix 1 well with ground meat; shell and cut eggs into pieces, set aside.

2 Wash rice, drain and add 2; bring to boil. Turn to low heat and cook for 40 minutes or until rice is very soft (for congee cooking time details, see note on p.79). Stir during cooking to prevent sticking. Add one ladle of rice to meat, mix well and return mixture to the pot. Stir to separate meat. Bring to boil, add 3 and bring to boil again. Turn off heat. Sprinkle with 4 and serve.

牛肉粥　BEEF CONGEE

【 廣東菜 】	【 4人份 】
牛肉 (切片)... 225公克 (6兩)	
1　醬油、酒...各⅔大匙	
玉米粉...1大匙	
2　蝦米 ...2大匙	
蒜(拍破)...2瓣	
醬油...½大匙	
3　米(長型米)...1杯	
水...10杯	
罐頭雞湯...2杯	
鹽...¾小匙	
胡椒...少許	
4　嫩薑絲...1大匙	
蔥絲...2大匙	
香菜末或芹菜末...4大匙	
炸餛飩皮絲或炸油條...1杯	

1 牛肉調①料拌醃，米洗淨。

2 油2大匙燒熱，炒香②料並加醬油，放入③料燒開，蓋鍋改小火煮40分鐘以上至米粒軟爛，中途需經常攪動以免黏鍋。最後將牛肉一片一片放入，肉熟後即熄火，撒上④料即可，趁熱食用。

■ 傳統的廣式粥品是用長型米熬煮1½小時以上至米粒碎爛，上面為家庭簡餐做法只煮40分鐘至米粒軟爛，熬煮時間可依個人喜好調整。④料是增添香味及口感之用，也可依個人喜好減化為一至兩種，若使用油條則先切小塊再炸。

【 CANTONESE CUISINE 】	【 SERVES 4 】
½ lb. (225g) beef, thinly sliced	
1　⅔ T. ea.: soy sauce, cooking wine	
1 T. cornstarch	
2　2 T. dried shrimp	
2 garlic cloves, smashed	
½ T. soy sauce	
3　1 c. long grain rice	
10 c. water	
2 c. canned chicken broth	
¾ t. salt	
dash of pepper	
4　1 T. shredded baby ginger root	
2 T. shredded green onion	
4 T. minced cilantro or celery	
1 c. strips of fried won ton skin	

1 Mix beef with ①. Wash and drain rice.

2 Heat 2 T. oil, stir-fry ② until fragrant. Add soy sauce to enhance flavor. Add ③, bring to boil; cover and cook over low heat for 40 minutes until rice is very soft. Stir during cooking to prevent sticking to the pot. Add beef, slice by slice, and cook only until meat changes color. Turn off heat, sprinkle with ④. Serve.

■ The traditional preparation of Cantonese congee calls for simmering long-grain rice for more than 1½ hours until the rice is broken and mashed. The above recipe requires simmering for only 40 minutes until the rice is softened. Simmering time can be lengthened according to the individual preferred texture of the congee. The ingredients in ④ are toppings for the congee, one, two, or all can easily complement the dish.

蘿蔔粥

【 4人份 】

1. 蝦米...2大匙
   蒜 (拍破)...2瓣
   油蔥酥...1大匙
   絞肉(豬或牛)...225公克(6兩)
   醬油...½大匙
   米...1杯
2. 罐頭雞湯...2杯
   水...6杯
   白蘿蔔絲...225公克(6兩)
3. 鹽...½小匙
   胡椒...¼小匙
4. 中式芹菜末、蔥花或香菜...2大匙

1 米洗淨

2 油2大匙燒熱，炒香1料，再入絞肉炒開，淋入醬油後隨入米略炒，續入2料燒開，改中火煮15分鐘至米熟軟，調入3料後隨意撒上4料即成。

■ 此為台灣家庭式的食譜，粥裡的材料如芋頭、絲瓜、竹筍或四季豆等可隨季節不同而選擇變化。

WHITE RADISH CONGEE

【 SERVES 4 】

1. 2 T. dried shrimp
   2 smashed garlic cloves
   1 T. fried shallots
   ½ lb. (225g) ground pork or beef
   ½ T. soy sauce
   1 c. rice
2. 2 c. canned chicken broth
   6 c. water
   ½ lb. (225g) shredded white radish
3. ½ t. salt
   ¼ t. pepper
4. 2 T. minced Chinese celery, green onion or cilantro

1 Wash and drain rice. Set aside.

2 Heat 2 T. oil, stir-fry 1 until fragrant. Add ground meat, stir to separate; add soy sauce to enhance flavor. Add in rice and stir lightly. Add 2 and bring to boil, turn to medium heat and cook for 15 minutes or until rice is cooked. Add 3 and sprinkle with 4. Serve.

■ Seasonal ingredients such as taro root, bamboo shoots may be added to this Taiwanese home-style dish for a variety of different flavors.

海鮮粥

【 4人份 】

熟蛤蜊肉*、蝦仁、魚肉
...共450公克 (12兩)

1 [酒...1大匙，薑末...½大匙

2 [米...1杯
煮蛤蜊湯汁...7杯
罐頭雞湯...2杯

3 [鹽...½小匙，胡椒...少許

4 [芹菜末或蔥末...2大匙
嫩薑絲 (無亦可)...2大匙

1　米洗淨。海鮮拌入1料備用。

2　將2料煮開，蓋鍋以小火滾煮15分鐘至米熟軟，放入魚、蝦煮至剛熟後加蛤蜊肉及3料熄火，食前撒上4料。

*　將新鮮蛤蜊洗淨放入滾水內(水宜蓋滿蛤蜊)，見蛤蜊殼一開即撈出，取出蛤蜊肉即為熟蛤蜊肉。煮過蛤蜊的湯汁濾去砂質再加水成7杯，即為蛤蜊湯汁。

■　海鮮料可自行選擇使用蟹、蚵或花枝。直接使用帶殼海鮮可簡化烹調過程，視覺上料多豐盛，但食用時較麻煩。

SEAFOOD CONGEE

【 SERVES 4 】

1 lb (450g) total: cooked clam meat*, shelled shrimp, fish fillets

1 [**1 T. cooking wine; ½ T. minced ginger root**

2 [**1 c. rice**
7 c. reserved liquid from cooking clams
2 c. canned chicken broth

3 [**½ t. salt**
dash of pepper

4 [**2 T. chopped celery or green onion**
2 T. shredded baby ginger root (optional)

1　Wash and drain rice. Mix seafood with 1.

2　Cook 2 until boiling, cover and turn heat to low. Cook 15 minutes or until rice is done. Add fish and shrimp; boil until almost cooked. Add clams and 3. Turn heat off. Sprinkle with 4 and serve.

*　Scrub and wash clams. Immerse clams in boiling water, cook until clams open and immediately remove from boiling water. Strain liquid through a sieve to remove any sand and reserve 7c. for 2. Remove meat from shells.

■　Crab, oyster, cuttlefish or other seafood ingredients may be added as desired. Adding seafood without removing the shells can simplify cooking procedures and make the dish look more sumptuous. This method however, does make more work for the diner.

米

麵 小菜

CHINESE RICE NOODLES APPETIZERS

SOUPS

SWEETS

簡餐 湯

甜點

雞絲涼麵　CHILLED CHICKEN NOODLES IN SESAME SAUCE

<table>
<tr><td>

【 2人份 】

帶骨雞肉...450公克(12兩)

蛋...2個

① 芝麻醬...3大匙
蒜泥...1小匙
糖、醋...各1大匙
醬油、麻油...各2大匙
雞高湯...7大匙，辣油...1大匙

乾麵...150公克(4兩)

② 小黃瓜絲、生菜絲、紅蘿蔔絲
...各½杯
香菜...少許

</td><td>

【 SERVES 2 】

1 lb. (450g) chicken (with bones)

2 eggs

3 T. sesame paste

1 t. ground garlic

1 T. ea.: sugar, vinegar

2 T. ea.: soy sauce, sesame oil

7 T. reserved chicken stock

1 T. chili oil

⅓ lb. (150g) dried noodles

½ c. ea.(shredded): cucumber, lettuce and carrot

cilantro as desired

</td></tr>
</table>

1 鍋內放入帶骨雞肉，加水滿過雞，水燒開後改中火煮約25分鐘取出，待冷去骨撕成絲，取雞絲150公克(4兩)，留7大匙雞高湯用在①料內，剩餘雞肉及雞湯可做其他用途。

2 蛋打散，鍋燒熱後在鍋面塗少許油，倒入打勻的蛋液，將鍋轉動成圓形，以小火煎至蛋皮邊翻起時翻面，煎至兩面呈金黃色即取出切絲。

3 將①料依序加入，邊加邊攪拌至無顆粒。

4 多量水燒開，將麵條煮熟後撈出，隨即用冷水漂涼後分成2份置於盤內，淋上適量①料後，分別擺上雞絲、蛋皮絲及②料即成。

■ 若在①料內加入適量的檸檬汁則味道更清香。

1 Place chicken in a pot, add water to cover chicken. Bring water to a boil; turn heat to medium and cook 25 minutes. Remove and let cool. Separate meat from the bones; shred meat into strips with hands to total ⅓ lb (150g). Reserve 7 T. chicken stock to use in ①. The remainder may be used for other purposes as desired.

2 Beat eggs. Heat wok and wipe on oil with a paper towel. Pour in beaten eggs and swirl them to create a thin pancake. Turn heat to low and cook until pancake edges curl; turn pancake over and cook other side until color turns brown; remove and shred.

3 Place ① in a bowl in the order listed stirring continuously until mixture is smooth.

4 Boil enough water to cook noodles; when cooked, remove and immerse in cold water immediately, then drain. Divide into two portions and put on separate plates. Pour on ①, add shredded chicken, shredded eggs and ② on each portion; serve.

■ Lemon juice may be added in ① to enhance the flavor.

麻醬麵

【 2人份 】

①
芝麻醬...3大匙
糖、醋...各½大匙
醬油、麻油...各2大匙
高湯或水...7大匙

②
蔥花...4大匙
香菜(切碎)...1大匙(無亦可)

乾麵...150公克(4兩)

1 將①料依序加入，邊加邊攪至無顆粒即成麻醬汁。

2 多量水燒開，將麵條煮熟後撈出分成兩份，分別淋上麻醬汁及②料後翻拌食用。

■ 麻醬汁是以芝麻醬及麻油為主拌成的(見①料)，風味單純、調理簡便且美味可口，可應用於各類麵點及涼拌菜上，是北方有名的調味醬汁之一。

NOODLES WITH SESAME SAUCE

【 SERVES 2 】

①
3 T. sesame paste
½ T. ea.: sugar, vinegar
2 T. ea.: soy sauce, sesame oil
7 T. stock or water

②
4 T. chopped green onion
1 T. chopped cilantro (optional)

⅓ lb. (150g) dried noodles

■ Sesame sauce as in ① is mainly made of sesame paste and sesame oil. This sauce has a pure sesame flavor and is easy to make. It is very popular in Northern China noodle dishes and with cold noodles.

1 Place ① in a bowl in the order listed, stirring continuously until mixture is smooth.

2 Boil enough water to cook the noodles; when cooked remove and divide into two portions and place in separate bowls. Pour on mixture ① and add ② to each portion. Mix and serve.

擔擔麵

【 2人份 】

1
- 芝麻醬...3大匙
- 糖、醋...各½大匙
- 醬油、麻油...各2大匙
- 高湯或水...7大匙

2
- 辣油、蒜末...各1小匙
- 花椒粉...¼小匙
- 蔥花...2大匙

乾麵...150公克(4兩)

1　將1料依序加入，邊加邊攪至無顆粒即成麻醬汁。

2　多量水燒開，將麵條煮熟後撈出分成兩份，分別拌入麻醬汁及2料食用。

■　擔擔麵是由小販挑著麵擔沿街叫賣得名，除了以麻醬汁為底外，還多加辣油、蒜末及花椒粉，另可隨喜好加入榨菜末及花生粉，吃時有麻辣口感，味道比麻醬麵濃郁，是四川有名的家常麵點。

SZECHWAN DAN-DAN NOODLES

【 SZECHWAN CUISINE 】

【 SERVES 2 】

1
- 3 T. sesame paste
- ½ T. ea.: sugar, vinegar
- 2 T. ea.: soy sauce, sesame oil
- 7 T. stock or water

2
- 1 t. ea.: chili oil, ground garlic
- ¼ t. Szechwan pepper powder
- 2 T. chopped green onion

⅓ lb. (150g) dried noodles

1　Place 1 in a bowl in the order listed, stirring continuously until mixture is smooth.

2　Boil enough water to cook the noodles. When cooked divide into two portions and place in separate bowls; pour 1 and add 2 to each portion, mix and serve.

■　"Dan-Dan Noodles" derives its name from the way this noodle dish was sold: street vendors carried small portable stands and hollered, "Dan-Dan Noodles," as they walked through neighborhoods. Besides sesame sauce as its base, a mixture of spicy oil, minced garlic, and Szechwan pepper powder make for an irresistibly aromatic yet spicy flavor. It is a famous Szechwan home-style noodle dish.

炸醬麵

【 北京菜 】

【 2人份 】

絞肉(豬、牛或雞)...225公克(6兩)	
洋蔥丁...1杯	
豆瓣醬*...3大匙	
1	水...½杯
	玉米粉...2小匙
	麻油...2小匙
	糖...1小匙
2	小黃瓜或其他蔬菜...切絲共3杯
	乾麵...150公克(4兩)

1　油3大匙燒熱，先炒香洋蔥，再將絞肉炒開至熟，隨入豆瓣醬炒香，再加 **1** 料燒開攪拌成濃稠狀即為炸醬。

2　多量水燒開，將麵條煮熟後撈出，分盛於兩個麵碗內，上擺 **2** 料及做好的炸醬，趁熱拌食。

＊　若無豆瓣醬可用醬油取代。

■　瘦肉丁與豆腐乾丁可取代絞肉來做炸醬，北方人喜歡在做好的炸醬麵內加數粒生蒜，可增加蒜的辛辣味。

SOY FLAVORED MEAT SAUCE OVER NOODLES

【 BEIJING CUISINE 】

【 SERVES 2 】

½ lb. (225g) ground pork, beef or chicken	
1 c. diced onions	
3 T. bean paste*	
1	½ c. water
	2 t. cornstarch
	2 t. sesame oil
	1 t. sugar
2	3 c. total (shredded): cucumber or other vegetables
	⅓ lb. (150g) dried noodles

1　Heat 3T. oil, stir-fry onions until fragrant; add meat and stir-fry until meat is separated and cooked. Add bean paste and stir-fry until fragrant; add **1** and bring to a boil, stir to thicken to make the meat sauce.

2　Boil enough water to cook noodles. Remove noodles when cooked and place in two separate bowls. Top each bowl with meat sauce and **2**. Mix and serve hot.

＊　If bean paste is not available, use soy sauce instead.

■　Diced lean meat and pressed bean curd may be used instead of ground meat. In Northern China, this dish is customarily served with several freshly peeled garlic cloves to enhance the spicy flavor.

切仔麵

【 2人份 】

豬腿肉...450公克(12兩)

油蔥酥...1大匙，醬油...½大匙

韭菜(切段)、豆芽菜...共3杯

1 煮肉湯...5杯，胡椒...⅛小匙

鹽、麻油...各1½小匙

台式油麵...450公克(12兩)

1 肉及6杯水放入鍋內燒開後，改小火蓋鍋煮20分鐘熄火，待降至常溫時撈出切片，留5杯湯汁用在1料內，多餘的肉片可沾蒜末醬油當小菜。

2 油蔥酥及油2大匙放入鍋內燒熱再放入醬油略炒，當香味溢出立即連油盛出。

3 韭菜及豆芽菜川燙撈出，分裝在2個麵碗內隨加入燒滾的1料。

4 水燒開，將麵川燙後撈起放入麵碗內，擺上肉片及淋入炒好的醬油蔥酥即成。

■ 切仔麵是台灣路邊小吃攤中常見的麵食，傳統的份量較少。切仔麵特別的地方是將麵裝入長柄竹勺內放入滾水中燙熱，竹勺子為"切仔"，所以切仔麵是因此而得名。

CHI-AH NOODLE SOUP

【 SERVES 2 】

1 lb. (450g) pork

1 T. fried shallots; ½ T. soy sauce

3 c. total: Chinese chives pieces, bean sprouts

1 | 5 c. reserved stock from cooking pork

1½ t. ea.: salt, sesame oil

⅛ t. pepper

1 lb. (450g) cooked Taiwanese noodles

1 Place meat and 6 c. water in a pot and bring to a boil. Cover and cook for 20 minutes over low heat; turn off heat. Let cool to room temperature; remove meat and slice. Reserve 5 c. pork stock for later use in 1. Any leftover meat may be dipped in soy sauce and minced garlic, as a tasty side dish.

2 Heat 2 T. oil and shallots; add soy sauce and stir-fry lightly, remove when aromatic.

3 Blanch chives and bean sprouts briefly, remove and divide into two large soup bowls. Boil 1 and pour into the bowls.

4 Boil water and blanch noodles, remove and put in the two bowls. Place sliced meat on noodles and pour soy sauce flavored shallots on top. Serve.

■ A very popular street food, this noodle dish is traditionally served in small portions. The name, "Chi-Ah" comes from the Taiwanese dialect describing a unique strainer used to cook the noodles, which is suitable for lowering into boiling water to warm the noodles. The strainer is small but deep enough to hold just one serving of noodles.

擔擔湯麵 | DAN-DAN NOODLE SOUP

<table>
<tr><td>【 2人份 】</td><td>[SERVES 2]</td></tr>
<tr><td>豬絞肉...150克(4兩)</td><td>⅓ lb. (150g) ground pork</td></tr>
<tr><td>甜麵醬...2大匙</td><td>2 T. sweet bean paste</td></tr>
<tr><td>青江菜...1棵(或豆芽菜2杯)</td><td>1 stalk of bok choy or 2 c. of bean sprouts</td></tr>
<tr><td>① 芝麻醬、水...各3大匙
糖、醋...各1小匙
醬油...2大匙</td><td>① 3 T. ea.: sesame paste, water
1 t. ea.: sugar, vinegar
2 T. soy sauce</td></tr>
<tr><td>② 罐頭雞湯...2杯
水...3杯</td><td>② 2 c. canned chicken broth
3 c. water</td></tr>
<tr><td>③ 蔥花...6大匙
花椒粉或胡椒...⅛小匙
香菜、辣油...隨意</td><td>③ 6 T. chopped green onions
⅛ t. Szechwan pepper powder or pepper
cilantro or chili oil as desired</td></tr>
<tr><td>乾麵...150公克(4兩)</td><td>⅓ lb (150g) dried noodles</td></tr>
</table>

1 鍋燒熱不放油,將絞肉炒約2分鐘至變白時,加入甜麵醬再炒1分鐘後盛起備用。青江菜直切成6瓣燙熟或將豆芽菜燙熟備用。

2 將①料依序加入攪拌均勻,分盛於2大碗內;將②料煮開後亦分盛於此2大碗內。

3 多量水燒開,將麵條煮熟後撈出,分盛於已裝湯的大碗內,上加蔬菜、肉末及③料。

■ 擔擔麵之類的小吃通常以小碗裝,家庭做時可分裝在2個大湯碗內供二人食用。

1 Heat wok with no oil; stir-fry meat for 2 minutes until it changes color. Add sweet bean paste and stir-fry for 1 minute, remove and set aside. Slice bok choy lengthwise to 6 pieces. Blanch bok choy or bean sprouts in boiling water, remove and set aside.

2 Mix ① in a bowl, in the order listed until smooth; divide and place in two separate large soup bowls. Boil ② and place in the bowls.

3 Boil enough water to cook noodles; remove the noodles when cooked and put in the two bowls. Add vegetables, meat and ③ on top of the noodles. Serve.

■ This popular street vendor's savory dish is usually served in small bowls. To serve at home as one-dish meals, use two large bowls for two servings.

酸辣肉絲湯麵 | HOT AND SOUR NOODLE SOUP

[四川菜]　　　　[2人份]

1 瘦肉絲(雞或豬)...150公克(4兩)

① ┌ 薑絲、辣椒醬...各1大匙
　　└ 酸菜*(切碎)...1杯
　　醬油...½大匙

② ┌ 罐頭雞湯...2杯
　　└ 水...3杯

③ ┌ 鹽、胡椒...各¼小匙
　　├ 糖、麻油...各½小匙
　　└ 胡椒...少許

青菜(略切)...225公克(6兩)

乾麵...150公克(4兩)

1 酸菜略沖洗去鹹味後擠乾，在乾鍋內稍微炒乾鏟出。

2 油3大匙燒熱，將①料依序放入炒香後，隨入肉絲炒開至變色，再入酸菜及醬油炒拌，加②料燒開改以中火煮5分鐘，酸菜鹹酸程度不同，試鹹淡再加③料，分盛在2個麵碗內。

3 多量水燒開，先將青菜燙熟撈出，再放入麵條煮熟撈出，分別放入麵碗內即可。

* 酸菜(圖1)是用大芥菜略曬後加鹽搓軟擠乾，放入罐內醃漬而成，酸菜可用於炒及煮湯。超市有現成的出售。

[SZECHWAN CUISINE]　　　　[SERVES 2]

⅓ lb. (150g) lean pork or chicken shreds

① ┌ 1 T. ea.: shredded ginger root, chili paste
　　└ 1 c. pickled mustard cabbage*, chopped
　　½ T. soy sauce

② ┌ 2 c. canned chicken broth
　　└ 3 c. water

③ ┌ ¼ t. ea.: salt, pepper
　　├ ½ t. ea.: sugar, sesame oil
　　└ dash of pepper

½ lb. (225g) green leafy vegetables, roughly cut

⅓ lb. (150g) dried noodles

1 Lightly wash mustard cabbage to remove salt then squeeze out excess water. Lightly stir-fry with no oil until dry; remove and set aside.

2 Heat 3 T. oil, add and stir-fry ① in the order listed, until fragrant. Add pork and stir-fry until meat is separated and color changes. Add the cabbage and soy sauce and mix well; add ② and bring to boil, turn to medium heat and cook for 5 minutes. Different brands of pickled cabbage have different degrees of saltiness. Taste soup to check for saltiness and then add ③. Place in two large soup bowls.

3 Boil water and blanch vegetables, remove and place in the two large soup bowls. Use remaining water to cook noodles. When cooked, remove the noodles and divide them into the two bowls and serve.

* To make Pickled Mustard Cabbage (Fig. 1): Slightly sun-dry mustard greens then mix with salt by hand to soften. Squeeze out excess water then keep in an air-tight container until pickled. It is suitable for stir-frying and making soup. Ready-made pickled mustard cabbage is available in markets.

雞腿湯麵　NOODLE SOUP WITH CRISPY CHICKEN LEGS

雞腿4隻...900公克 (1½斤)

① 玉米粉、醬油...各1½大匙
糖、酒...各½大匙
鹽...½小匙
五香粉或胡椒...⅓小匙

蛋(打散)...1個

玉米粉...4大匙

酸菜(見93頁)...1½杯

炸油...適量

② 辣椒絲...½大匙
鹽、糖...各½小匙
麻油...½小匙

③ 蔥末、醬油...各2大匙
胡椒、麻油...各少許

④ 罐頭雞湯...4杯
水...6杯

乾麵...300公克 (8兩)

1　雞腿在順骨二側劃刀(易入味也容易炸熟)，加①料拌勻。炸前拌入蛋，再沾上玉米粉。

2　酸菜切絲泡水5分鐘，握乾水份以去鹹味。油2大匙燒熱，放入酸菜略炒，再入②料炒勻盛出。

3　炸油燒熱，將雞腿炸至表面略凝固成形後，改中火炸8分鐘至肉熟、表面酥脆呈金黃色撈出。

4　將③料分盛於4個麵碗裡，④料燒開亦加入麵碗內。

5　多量水燒開，將麵條煮熟也分盛於碗內，上加酸菜及炸雞腿即成。

排骨湯麵　用炸排骨4片 (見67頁)取代炸雞腿4隻，即成排骨湯麵。

4 chicken thighs, about 2 lbs. (900g)

① 1½ T. ea.: cornstarch, soy sauce
½ T. ea.: sugar, cooking wine
½ t. salt
⅓ t. five spice powder or pepper

1 egg, lightly beaten

4 T. cornstarch

1½ c. pickled mustard cabbage (p. 93)

Oil for deep frying

② ½ T. shredded red chili pepper
½ t. ea.: salt, sugar
½ t. sesame oil

③ 2 T. ea.: chopped green onions, soy sauce
dash of pepper and sesame oil

④ 4 c. canned chicken broth
6 c. water

⅔ lb. (300g) dried noodles

1　Score sides of chicken legs to absorb seasoning and for faster frying. Mix with ①. Dip in beaten egg then cornstarch before deep-frying.

2　Soak cabbage in water for 5 minutes; squeeze out excess water to remove salt. Heat 2 T. oil, stir-fry cabbage briefly; add ② and mix well. Remove and set aside.

3　Heat oil for deep frying and fry chicken over high heat until coating is firm; lower heat to medium and fry 8 minutes until chicken is crispy and golden. Remove and set aside.

4　Put ③ in each of four large soup bowls. Boil ④ and divide into the four bowls.

5　Boil enough water to cook the noodles. When cooked remove and divide the noodles into the four bowls. Place the cabbage and chicken on top of the noodles. Serve.

NOODLE SOUP WITH FRIED PORK CHOPS Use 4 pork chops (p.67) in place of chicken thighs, all the other ingredients and procedures are the same as above.

雪菜肉絲麵　　RAPE GREENS AND PORK NOODLE SOUP

<table>
<tr><td rowspan="3">①</td><td>瘦肉絲(豬、或雞)...150公克(4兩)</td></tr>
<tr><td>醬油、酒、玉米粉...各½大匙</td></tr>
</table>

【 2人份 】

瘦肉絲(豬、或雞)...150公克(4兩)

① 醬油、酒、玉米粉...各½大匙

雪菜*(切碎)...1½杯

蔥白、辣椒末...共1大匙

② 水...1大匙
鹽...⅓小匙
糖、麻油...各1小匙
胡椒...少許

③ 罐頭雞湯...2杯
水...3杯

醬油...½大匙

乾麵...150 公克(4兩)

1 肉加①料拌勻；雪菜沖洗擠乾在鍋內略炒乾盛出。

2 油2大匙燒熱，先炒香蔥及辣椒再入肉絲炒開，隨入雪菜及②料炒勻即盛出。

3 將③料燒開加醬油，分別放入2個麵碗內。

4 多量水燒開，將麵放入滾水中，煮熟後撈出也分別放入麵碗內，再加上雪菜肉絲即成。

* 雪菜(圖1) 的作法為450公克(12兩)的油菜或白蘿蔔莖葉洗淨瀝乾，撒上1大匙鹽，揉搓至軟，醃一天以上，使用前略洗，擠乾水份，剁碎即可使用 。

【 SERVES 2 】

⅓ lb. (150g) shredded lean pork or chicken

① ½ T. ea.: soy sauce, cooking wine, cornstarch

1½ c. chopped salted rape greens* (Fig. 1)

1 T. total: chopped white part of green onion,
red chili pepper,

② 1 T. water; ⅛ t. salt
1 t. ea.: sugar, sesame oil
dash of pepper

③ 2 c. canned chicken broth
3 c. water

½ T. soy sauce

⅓ lb. (150g) dried noodles

1 Mix pork with ①. Lightly wash rape greens and squeeze out excess water; place in a wok with no oil and stir-fry until dry. Set aside.

2 Heat 2 T. oil and stir-fry green onions and chili until fragrant. Add shredded meat and stir-fry until meat is separated and cooked; put in greens and ②, mix well. Remove and set aside.

3 Boil ③, add soy sauce; divide and place in two large soup bowls.

4 Boil enough water to cook noodles; when cooked, remove and divide the noodles into two large soup bowls. Put greens and meat on top of the noodles and serve.

* To make salted rape greens, wash and squeeze dry 1 lb. (450g) rape greens or the greens of the white radish (stems and leaves). Sprinkle 1 T. salt and rub into the vegetable until it softens. Marinate for at least one day. To use, rinse and squeeze dry, then chop to bits.

肉燥擔仔麵

【 2人份 】

蝦...6隻	
韭菜(切段)、豆芽菜...各1杯	
1	罐頭雞湯...2杯
	水...3杯
	醋、麻油...各½小匙
	鹽、胡椒...各⅛小匙
2	肉燥及滷汁...共1杯(見51頁)
	蒜末...1大匙
	台式油麵*... 450公克(12兩)

1 蝦燙熟後去殼留尾。

2 韭菜,豆芽菜分別放入滾水中川燙熟撈出分裝在2個碗內,加入燒開的**1**料。

3 多量水燒開,將麵放入滾水中,川燙後撈起也分別置於碗內,加上**2**料及蝦即成。

* 傳統擔仔麵使用台式油麵,若無油麵,可用乾麵150公克(4兩)煮熟後取代。

DAN-TZE NOODLES

【 SERVES 2 】

6 shrimp	
1 c. ea.: Chinese chives sections, bean sprouts	
1	**2 c. canned chicken broth**
	3 c. water
	½ t. ea.: vinegar, sesame oil
	⅛ t. ea.: salt, pepper
2	**1 c. total: savory meat sauce (p. 51)**
	1 T. minced garlic
	1 lb. (450g) cooked Taiwanese noodles*

1 Boil shrimp until done; shell the shrimp but leave the tail intact.

2 Separately blanch chives and bean sprouts; remove and place both in two large soup bowls. Boil **1** and divide into the two large soup bowls.

3 Boil enough water to blanch noodles briefly; remove and divide the noodles to the two bowls. Put **2** and the shrimp on top of noodles. Serve.

* Traditional Dan-Tze Noodles are made from Taiwanese noodles. If Taiwanese noodles are not available, cook ⅓ lb. (150g) dried noodles as a replacement.

榨菜肉絲麵

【 2人份 】

瘦肉絲(豬、牛或雞)
...150公克(4兩)

① 醬油、酒、玉米粉...各½大匙
蔥白...6段，榨菜絲*...¾杯

② 水...1大匙，醬油...½大匙
糖、麻油...各1小匙
鹽、胡椒....各¼小匙

③ 罐頭雞湯...2杯，水...3杯
青菜(切段)...150公克(4兩)
乾麵...150 公克(4兩)

1　肉加①料拌勻。榨菜絲因味鹹宜
泡水10分鐘後擠乾水份再使用。

2　油2大匙燒熱，將蔥炒香，放
入肉絲炒開至熟，加入榨菜及
②料拌炒均勻盛出。

3　將③料燒開分別盛在2個麵碗
內。

4　多量水燒開，先將青菜放入燙
熟撈出，再入麵條煮熟撈出連
同青菜分別放入麵碗內，最後
放上榨菜肉絲即成。

＊　榨菜(圖1)是芥菜莖加鹽、香料
與辣椒粉醃漬晒乾而成。

MUSTARD GREENS AND PORK NOODLE SOUP

[SERVES 2]

⅓ lb. (150g) shredded lean pork, beef, or chicken

① ½ T. ea.: soy sauce, cooking wine, cornstarch

6 pieces white part of green onion

¾ c. shredded Szechwan pickled mustard greens*

② 1 T. water; ½ T. soy sauce
1 t. ea.: sugar, sesame oil
¼ t. ea.: salt, pepper

③ 2 c. canned chicken broth; 3 c. water
⅓ lb. (150g) any green vegetables, cut into pieces
⅓ lb. (150g) dried noodles

1　Mix meat with ①. Soak mustard greens in water for 10 minutes to reduce salt, squeeze out excess water before use.

2　Heat 2 T. oil; stir-fry green onions until fragrant. Add shredded meat and stir-fry until meat separates and is cooked. Add mustard greens and ②, mix well; set aside.

3　Boil ③, divide into two large soup bowls.

1

4　Blanch vegetables in boiling water; remove. Cook noodles in boiling water, remove when cooked, put the noodles, then the vegetables in the soup bowls. Place meat and mustard greens on top of the noodles and serve.

＊　Szechwan pickled mustard greens (Fig.1) are made by preserving stems of mustard greens with salt, spices and chili powder, then sun-dried.

清燉牛肉麵

【 4人份 】

牛腩或牛腱...900公克 (1½斤)	
薑...10片，蔥...2枝	
① 胡椒、鹽...各½小匙	
酒...3大匙	
水...10杯，罐頭雞湯...4杯	
八角...1朵，麻油...½大匙	
乾麵...300公克(8兩)	

1　牛肉切塊(圖1)，在滾水內川燙撈出後，放入①料內翻炒燒煮5分鐘至汁快收乾，再加水及雞湯燒開去除泡沫加入八角蓋鍋，改小火燒煮約2小時，至肉熟軟湯汁剩8杯。淋入麻油，分盛4個麵碗內。

2　多量水燒開，將麵條煮熟後撈出，也分別放入4個麵碗內，隨喜好加入燙熟青菜即成。

■　牛肉因產地的不同，燒煮的時間由1小時至3小時不等。講究的清燉牛肉做法除用牛腩外多加乾干貝及老母雞，湯汁鮮美不需另加罐頭雞湯，以燉的方式來烹調，燉後老母雞取出不要。

NOODLES IN CLEAR BEEF BROTH

【 SERVES 4 】

2 lbs. (900g) beef brisket or beef shank	
10 ginger root slices; 2 green onions	
① ½ t. ea.: pepper, salt	
3 T. cooking wine	
10 c. water; 4 c. canned chicken broth	
1 star anise	
½ T. sesame oil	
⅔ lb. (300g) dried noodles	

1

1　Cut beef into 1½" (4 cm) chunks (Fig. 1) and blanch in boiling water; remove and stir-fry with ①. Cook for 5 minutes until liquid is almost evaporated. Add water and chicken broth, bring to a boil; use a spoon to skin the foam off the surface of the broth. Add star anise, cover and cook over low heat for two hours until meat is soft and liquid is reduced to 8 c. Add sesame oil and divide into four large soup bowls.

2　Boil enough water to cook noodles; when cooked, put them into the four bowls. Green leafy vegetables may be added as desired.

■　The beef may require one to three hours of cooking depending on the beef's origin. For the truly discriminating connoisseur of "Clear Beef Broth", choice beef brisket is accompanied by dried scallops and an aged hen. The resulting broth is so flavorful and delicious that canned chicken broth will not be necessary; discard the chicken when done.

海鮮湯麵

【 2人份 】

	海參...150公克(4兩)
1	薑...2片，酒...1大匙，水...2杯
	魷魚...150公克(4兩)
	蝦...6隻
	蔥白...4段
2	醬油...½大匙
	鹽...½小匙，酒...1大匙
3	罐頭雞湯...2杯，水...3杯
	青菜...6把
	乾麵...150公克(4兩)

1　海參切塊，以 1 料燒煮去腥味後撈出(煮過的湯汁不要)，魷魚切塊*，蝦去殼及腸泥。

2　油4大匙燒熱，先炒蔥段，再將海參、魷魚、蝦及 2 料依序放入略炒，再加入 3 料及青菜燒開後，將材料先撈出，湯汁分盛2個麵碗內。

3　多量水燒開，將麵煮熟分盛在麵碗內，上加煮好的材料即成。

*　魷魚切法：魷魚切約4公分寬長條，斜切條紋，再由另一邊斜切成交叉紋(圖1)後切塊。

SEAFOOD NOODLE SOUP

【 SERVES 2 】

	⅓ lb. (150g) sea cucumber
1	2 slices ginger root
	1 T. cooking wine; 2 c. water
	⅓ lb. (150g) squid; 6 shrimp
	4 pieces white part of green onion
2	½ T. soy sauce; ½ t. salt; 1 T. cooking wine
3	2 c. canned chicken broth; 3 c. water
	6 branches green leafy vegetables
	⅓ lb. (150g) dried noodles

1　Cut sea cucumber into 1½" (4 cm) chunks, blanch in 1 to remove any odor. Discard liquid. Cut squid into pieces*. Shell, then devein shrimp.

2　Heat 4 T. oil, stir-fry onions until fragrant; add sea cucumber, squid, shrimp and 2, in that order, stir-frying during the process. Add 3 and vegetables, bring to boil. Remove all ingredients and pour remaining soup into two large soup bowls.

1

3　Boil enough water to cook noodles, remove noodles when cooked. Divide into the two bowls, then add all the cooked ingredients on top. Serve.

*　Cut squid into 1½" (4 cm) wide strips. Score diagonally to form crisscross cuts (Fig. 1), then cut them into pieces.

紅燒牛肉麵　BRAISED BEEF NOODLE SOUP

【 4人份 】

牛肉*...900公克 (1½斤)

① ┌ 蔥(切段)...6枝
  └ 薑...6片，蒜頭...3瓣

② ┌ 豆瓣醬...1½大匙
  │ 辣豆瓣醬(或辣椒醬)...1½小匙
  └ 醬油...¾杯

③ ┌ 水...8杯，酒...2大匙
  └ 糖...1大匙，八角...2朵

④ ┌ 蔥花...2大匙
  │ 醬油...2大匙
  │ 麻油...2小匙
  └ 胡椒...少許

青菜...300公克 (8兩)

乾麵... 300公克 (8兩)

1　牛肉切塊。

2　油2大匙燒熱，將①、②料依序放入炒香，再入③料及牛肉燒開，去除泡沫，蓋鍋改小火續煮1小時至肉熟軟，湯汁剩6杯時將肉撈出，再加水6杯煮開待用。

3　在4個麵碗內分別放入 料及牛肉湯汁。

4　多量水燒開，先將青菜燙熟撈出，再入麵條煮熟撈出，分別放入麵碗內。上加牛肉即成。可隨意搭配酸菜配食。

*　可使用略帶點肥肉或筋的牛肉，如牛腩、肋條、牛腱(圖1)等來烹煮；牛肉因產地不同，燒煮時間由1小時至3小時不等。

■　紅燒牛肉麵是很受歡迎的中式麵食之一，市面上有許多麵館及小攤販以紅燒牛肉麵為招牌吸引饕客賞光。除了辣味的紅燒牛肉麵之外，還有不辣的清燉牛肉麵，通常搭配各式滷味小菜一同販賣，成為特殊的牛肉麵文化。

【 SERVES 4 】

2 lbs. (900g) beef brisket or beef shank*

① ┌ 6 pieces green onion
  └ 6 slices ginger root, 3 garlic cloves

② ┌ 1½ T. bean paste
  │ 1½ t. hot bean paste or chili paste
  └ ¾ c. soy sauce

③ ┌ 8 c. water; 2 T. cooking wine
  └ 1 T. sugar; 2 star anise

④ ┌ 2 T. chopped green onion
  │ 2 T. soy sauce
  │ 2 t. sesame oil
  └ dash of pepper

⅔ lb. (300g) any green leafy vegetables

⅔ lb. (300g) dried noodles

1　Cut beef into 1½" (4 cm) chunks.

2　Heat 2 T. oil, add ① and ② in the order listed. Stir-fry until fragrant; add ③ and beef, bring to boil. Use a spoon to skim foam from surface. Cover and simmer over low heat for one hour until meat is soft and liquid is reduced to 6 c. Remove meat and set aside. Add 6 c. of water and bring to boil then turn off heat.

3　Divide ④ and liquid into four large soup bowls.

4　Blanch vegetables in plenty of boiling water and remove. Use the boiling water to cook noodles; remove noodles when cooked. Divide noodles and vegetables into the four bowls. Add the cooked beef to each bowl and serve with pickled mustard greens if desired.

*　Select beef with some fat or with some tendon, such as beef shank (Fig. 1), tendon, or flank. The beef may require one to three hours of cooking depending on the cut and where the beef was produced.

■　"Braised Beef Noodle Soup" is a highly popular Chinese noodle dish. Many noodle shops and street vendors use this dish to draw diners to their establishments. In addition to the spicy, braised beef noodle soup variety, there is also the clear broth style. Noodle soups are often accompanied by braised side dishes, thus making the enjoyment of beef noodle soup a custom of its own.

蝦茸窩麵

【 4人份 】

蝦仁、雞肉*...(剁碎)300公克(8兩)

1｜ 酒...1大匙，鹽、麻油...各1小匙

2｜ 蛋白...3個，水3大匙

3｜ 筍片、洋菇片...共2杯
　　罐頭雞湯...4杯，水...6杯

4｜ 玉米粉、水...各8大匙

5｜ 醬油...2大匙，胡椒...¼小匙
　　麻油、糖...各1小匙
　　蔥末、薑末...各1大匙

乾麵...300公克(8兩)

1　蝦、雞茸拌入①料後，將②料分次加入攪拌。若用攪拌機則將蝦、雞茸與①、②料全部一起加入攪拌成糊狀備用。

2　將③料燒開，以④料勾芡成糊狀，用大勺舀出湯放入蝦、雞茸攪散，再放回湯內攪拌燒開，熄火拌入⑤料即成蝦茸濃湯。

3　多量水燒開，放入麵條煮熟後撈出，分盛在4個碗內，加上做好的蝦茸濃湯即成。

*　蝦及雞肉的比例沒有限制，也可僅用一種。因蝦或雞均已剁碎，若用麵線取代乾麵，則適合老人及小孩食用。

MINCED SHRIMP CHOWDER WITH NOODLES

【 SERVES 4 】

⅔ lb. (300g) total: shrimp, ground chicken*

1｜ 1 T. cooking wine
　　1 t. ea.: salt, sesame oil

2｜ 3 egg whites; 3 T. water

3｜ 2 c. total: sliced bamboo shoot and mushrooms
　　4 c. canned chicken broth; 6 c. water

4｜ 8 T. ea.: cornstarch, water

5｜ 2 T. soy sauce; ¼ t. pepper
　　1 t. ea.: sesame oil, sugar
　　1 T. ea. (minced): green onion, ginger root

⅔ lb. (300g) dried noodles

1　Mince shrimp and chicken; mix in ①. Gradually add ② and stir simultaneously until mixed well. If food processor is used, you can add ① and ② at the same time. Mixture should have a thick consistency.

2　Bring ③ to a boil, add mixture ④ to thicken. Use a ladle to scoop some soup to the shrimp and chicken mixture; mix well and return it to the soup. Bring to a boil, turn off heat and mix in ⑤.

3　Boil enough water to cook noodles, when cooked, remove noodles and divide noodles to four large soup bowls. Add shrimp chicken soup on top of noodles and serve.

*　Use shrimp or chicken or both, depending on personal preferences or availability. Since the chicken and shrimp are ground, substituting noodles with somen will make the dish easier to eat by children and the elderly.

炒馬湯麵

【 2人份 】

1 魷魚(切花)、蝦仁、豬或雞肉絲
　　…共225公克(6兩)

2 蒜末…½大匙，乾辣椒(略切)…3條
　蝦米、紅椒粉(圖1)…各1大匙
　醬油…1大匙

3 洋蔥、高麗菜、紅蘿蔔
　　…(切絲)共225公克(6兩)

4 罐頭雞湯…2杯，水…3杯

5 鹽…¼小匙
　糖、酒、麻油…各¾小匙
　乾麵…150公克(4兩)

1 油2大匙燒熱，將1料內的材料
　炒至魷魚捲曲肉變色即盛出。

2 油2大匙燒熱，依序放入2料用
　中火炒香，隨入醬油及3料略
　炒，再加入4料燒開至蔬菜略
　軟，最後放入5料及炒好的1料
　即為三鮮湯。

3 多量水燒開，將麵放入滾水中，
　煮熟後撈起置於2個碗中，加入
　三鮮湯即可。

■ 炒馬麵有湯麵和乾麵兩種，特色
　是加入紅椒粉及乾辣椒，使煮出
　來的麵色略紅並帶有辛辣口感。

SPICY SEAFOOD NOODLE SOUP

【 SERVES 2 】

1　½ lb. (225g) total: squid, shelled shrimp, shredded pork or chicken

2　½ T. minced garlic
　3 dried red chili peppers, cut into pieces
　1 T. ea.: dried shrimp, red chili powder (Fig. 1)
　1 T. soy sauce

3　½ lb. (225g) total (shredded): onion, cabbage, carrot

4　2 c. canned chicken broth; 3 c. water

5　¼ t. salt
　¾ t. ea.: sugar, cooking wine, sesame oil
　⅓ lb. (150g) dried noodles

1 Heat 2T. oil, stir-fry 1 until squid is curled and meat changes color; remove and set aside.

2 Heat 2T. oil, stir-fry 2 over medium heat until fragrant. Add soy sauce and 3; stir-fry briefly. Add 4 and bring to a boil; cook until vegetables are slightly soft. Add 5 and 1 to complete the

seafood, meat and vegetable soup, set aside.

3 Boil enough water to cook noodles; when noodles are cooked divide into two large soup bowls. Pour the soup and ingredients on the noodles. Serve.

■ "Spicy Seafood Noodles" can be served as noodle soup or stir-fried noodles. The red chili powder and dried chilies lightly color and add spiciness to the noodles.

麵疙瘩

【 北京菜 】

【 2人份 】

麵粉...1杯

水...½杯

① 蔥白...8段，蝦米...3大匙
豬或雞肉片...225公克(6兩)

醬油...1大匙

水...5杯

② 鹽...1小匙
胡椒、麻油...各¼小匙

蔥花...隨意

1　將麵粉放入盆內加水用筷子攪拌均勻後，表面略抹上油，蓋上保鮮膜醒20分鐘。

2　油3大匙燒熱，將①料依序放入炒香，肉變色即加醬油，並入水燒開後，手沾些油依想要的大小將麵糰撕下一片片放入鍋內(圖1)，煮至麵片浮起，加入②料撒上蔥花即可。

■　麵疙瘩看似麻煩其實很簡單，只要有麵粉再湊一湊冰箱內現成的肉及蔬菜，即可做一頓簡餐；現做的麵片，不用高湯也鮮美好吃。

HOME-MADE NOODLE SOUP WITH GREEN ONIONS
[BEIJING CUISINE]

[SERVES 2]

1 c. flour; ½ c. water

① 8 sections of white part of green onion; 3 T. dried shrimp
½ lb. (225g) pork or chicken slices

1 T. soy sauce; 5 c. water

② 1 t. salt
¼ t. ea.: pepper, sesame oil

chopped green onions as desired

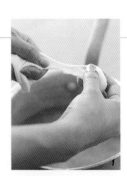

1　Put flour into a bowl, add water and mix well to make dough. Rub oil on surface of the dough; cover and let sit 20 minutes.

2　Heat 3 T. oil, add and stir-fry ① in the order listed until fragrant and meat changes color. Immediately add soy sauce and water and bring to boil. Rub some oil on hands to keep them from sticking to the dough; tear off a small piece of dough, size as desired (Fig. 1), and put it into boiling water. Continue with remaining dough. Cook until dough floats to the surface. Add ②, sprinkle on onions and serve.

■　While this dish may appear hard to prepare, it is actually quite easy. All that is required is flour and whatever meats and vegetables are in the refrigerator to make a quick meal. The hand-made noodle pieces are very tasty without having to use stock to enhance the flavor.

牛肉鍋燒麵

【 2人份 】

1. 蔥...4枝
   番茄(切塊)...1個

2. 罐頭雞湯...2杯，水...4杯
   醬油...1大匙，胡椒...⅛小匙
   糖、鹽、麻油...各½小匙

3. 牛肉片...150公克(4兩)
   草菇、魚丸...各6個
   茼蒿菜...150公克(4兩)

   熟烏龍麵...450公克(12兩)
   砂鍋...2個

1 多量水燒開，將烏龍麵放入滾水中川燙後撈出；蔥切段分蔥白及蔥綠備用。

2 分別將所有材料分成二份。

3 兩個砂鍋內分別放入油1大匙，取1份1料略炒，隨加2料燒滾，再放入麵及3料，蓋鍋燒滾即可。

■ 砂鍋加熱較慢但保溫性佳，可直接煮好端出，適合在寒冷的冬天食用。

BEEF HOT POT WITH NOODLES

【 SERVES 2 】

1. 4 green onions; 1 tomato cut in pieces

2. 2 c. canned chicken broth; 4 c. water
   1 T. soy sauce; ⅛ t. pepper
   ½ t. ea.: sugar, salt, sesame oil

3. ⅓ lb. (150g) beef (thin slices)
   6 ea.: straw mushrooms, fish balls
   ⅓ lb. (150g) tong ho

   1 lb. (450g) cooked udon
   2 clay pots

1 Boil enough water to blanch udon and drain. Cut green onions into pieces, separating white from green.

2 Divide all ingredients into two portions.

3 Pour 1 T. oil into a clay pot. Take one portion of each of the previously divided ingredients for each clay pot. Stir-fry 1 briefly; add 2 and bring to boil. Add noodles and 3, cover and bring to boil. Follow same procedures for second clay pot. Serve.

■ A clay pot takes longer to heat food, but can keep food warm longer. This dish is traditionally served in a clay pot during cold winters.

大滷麵　DA-LU NOODLE CHOWDER

[北京菜]　　　[2人份]　　　　[BEIJING CUISINE]　　　[SERVES 2]

瘦肉片(豬、牛或雞)...150公克(4兩)	⅓ lb. (150g) sliced pork, beef or chicken
① 醬油、玉米粉...各1小匙	① 1 t. ea.: soy sauce, cornstarch
② 木耳絲、香菇絲...各¼杯	② ¼ c. ea.(softened in water, shredded): black wood ears, black mushrooms
番茄塊...1杯	1 c. tomato (cut into pieces)
醬油...1大匙	1 T. soy sauce
③ 罐頭雞湯...2杯	③ 2 c. canned chicken broth; 3 c. water
水...3杯	
筍片、金針...各½杯	½ c. ea.: bamboo shoot slices, dried lily buds
鹽...¼小匙	¼ t. salt
麻油、胡椒...各少許	dash of sesame oil and pepper
④ 玉米粉...3大匙	④ 3 T. cornstarch
水...5大匙	5 T. water
蛋(打散)...2個	2 eggs, slightly beaten
青江菜(略切)...150公克(4兩)	⅓ lb. (150g) bok choy, roughly cut
乾麵...150公克(4兩)	⅓ lb. (150g) dried noodles

1　肉片加①料調勻，用2大匙的油，先炒香②料再將肉炒開至變色盛出。

2　油2大匙燒熱，先炒番茄續入醬油及③料燒開，放回炒熟肉片，再以④料勾芡成薄糊狀，最後把蛋汁徐徐倒入，見蛋花浮出湯面即熄火，分盛在2個麵碗內。

3　多量水燒開，將青菜燙熟撈出，再放入麵條煮熟撈出，各分盛在麵碗內即可。

■　大滷麵以材料豐富可隨意變化為特色，食時可酌加少許辣豆瓣醬或蒜末，味道更佳。

1　Marinate pork in ①. Heat 2 T. oil, stir-fry ② until fragrant; stir-fry pork until meat is separated and changes color, remove.

2　Heat 2 T. oil.　Stir-fry tomatoes, add soy sauce and ③; bring to a boil, return cooked meat. Stir ④ to thicken, pour eggs into the broth in a slow stream; stir then turn off heat when egg flakes float to top. Divide into two large soup bowls.

3　Blanch vegetables in boiling water and remove. Use the boiling water to cook noodles; remove noodles when cooked. Place noodles and vegetables in the two bowls. Serve.

■　"Da-Lu Noodle Chowder" draws on an assortment of ingredients which may be varied according to preference. Adding some hot bean paste or minced garlic can greatly enhance the taste.

香菇肉羹麵　PORK AND MUSHROOM NOODLE CHOWDER

【　台灣菜　】　　　　　　【　2人份　】

<table>
</table>

瘦肉(豬或雞)...150公克(4兩)

1 ⎡ 醬油、玉米粉...各½大匙

魚漿...150公克(4兩)

油蔥酥...1大匙

香菇(泡軟、切絲)...2朵

醬油...1½大匙

2 ⎡ 罐頭筍絲、紅蘿蔔絲...共1杯

罐頭雞湯...2杯

└ 水...3杯

3 ⎡ 玉米粉...3大匙

└ 水...3大匙

4 ⎡ 糖...½大匙

烏醋...1大匙

└ 麻油、胡椒...各少許

台式油麵...450公克(12兩)

香菜末...½杯

【　TAIWANESE CUISINE　】　　　　【　SERVES 2　】

⅓ lb. (150g) lean pork or chicken

1 ⎡ ½ T. ea.: soy sauce, cornstarch

⅓ lb. (150g) fish paste

1 T. fried shallots

2 black mushrooms, softened in water and shredded

1½ T. soy sauce

2 ⎡ 1 c. total: canned bamboo shoot shreds,
　　　shredded carrots

2 c. canned chicken broth

└ 3 c. water

3 ⎡ 3 T. ea.: cornstarch, water

4 ⎡ ½ T. sugar

1 T. black vinegar

└ dash of sesame oil, pepper

1lb. (450g) cooked Taiwanese noodles

½ c. chopped cilantro

---

1 肉切片，先調上 1 料，再加入魚漿拌勻備用。

2 油2大匙燒熱，炒香油蔥酥及香菇，隨入醬油及 2 料，不需等到湯滾開即將拌好的肉片一片片投入，待湯燒開肉片浮起，再以 3 料勾芡即熄火，加入 4 料調味，即為肉羹。

3 多量水燒開，將麵煮熟後撈出置於兩個麵碗中，淋上肉羹及撒上香菜即成。

■ 肉羹麵不加麵條時可用來當湯，常與肉燥飯(見51頁)配食，為傳統的台灣小吃。

---

1 Slice meat and marinate in 1; mix meat with fish paste.

2 Heat 2 T. oil, stir-fry shallots and mushrooms until fragrant. Add soy sauce and then 2. Add in meat mixture, piece by piece, cook until liquid boils and meat floats. Add mixed 3 to thicken soup; turn off heat. Add 4 to desired taste.

3 Boil enough water to blanch noodles; remove them to two large soup bowls. Pour the thick soup over the noodles and sprinkle on cilantro. Serve.

■ This dish may be served without noodles. It is a popular Taiwanese street vendor food and is commonly served with "Savory Meat Sauce over Rice" (p.51) when noodles are not used.

台式米粉湯

【 2人份 】

①	蝦皮*...1大匙，醬油...1大匙
	蔥白(3公分長)...4段
	香菇(切絲)...2朵
	瘦肉絲...150公克(4兩)
	水...6杯
②	紅蘿蔔絲、高麗菜絲 ...共225公克(6兩)
	鹽...1小匙
	胡椒、麻油...各¼小匙
	乾米粉...50公克(1.5兩)

1 米粉略沖洗浸泡5分鐘撈出備用。

2 油3大匙燒熱，依序將①料炒香，隨入水燒開後加②料再燒開，最後加入米粉，待米粉熟了即可熄火。

* 蝦皮是小蝦曬乾的。若無可用蝦米或魚乾取代。一般家庭常用這種乾貨做菜來補助湯汁之鮮美，不另準備高湯，此為家庭簡便米粉湯之做法。

■ 米粉種類可任選，因米粉易吸湯汁，需準備充份的湯水，又因不耐煮，要隨時留意米粉的熟軟度。

TAIWANESE RICE VERMICELLI SOUP

[SERVES 2]

①	1 T. dried shrimp skin*; 1 T. soy sauce
	4 white pieces of green onion, 1¼" (3 cm)
	2 black mushrooms, softened in water and shredded
	⅓ lb. (150g) lean pork, shredded or sliced
	6 c. water
②	½ lb. (225g) total (shredded): carrots, cabbage
	1 t. salt
	¼ t. ea.: pepper, sesame oil
	1⅔ oz (50g) dried rice vermicelli

1 Lightly wash rice vermicelli and then soak in water for five minutes; remove and set aside.

2 Heat 3 T. oil; add and stir-fry ① in the order listed until fragrant. Add water and bring to boil. Add ② and bring to boil again, then add rice vermicelli and cook. When vermicelli is cooked turn off heat. Serve.

* If dried shrimp skins are not available, dried shrimp or dried small fish may be substituted. Dried seafood is commonly used to flavor soups instead of using stock. This is an easy way to prepare family-style rice noodle soup.

■ Rice noodles come in a great variety suiting almost any preference. Because rice noodles are very absorbent, they require plenty of water/broth. Rice noodles also overcook easily and can become too soft; therefore constant monitoring of doneness is necessary.

干燒伊麵

【 2人份 】

1 {
薑絲...1小匙
香菇...2朵
}

2 {
蠔油...2大匙
醬油...½大匙
高湯...½杯
胡椒...少許
}

3 {
豆芽菜、韭黃(切段)、甜椒絲
　　...共150公克(4兩)
}

伊麵... 2包(100g)

1 香菇泡軟切絲，2料調好備用。

2 多量水燒開，放入麵條，見麵條軟立即撈出備用。

3 油2大匙燒熱，先將1料炒香，再入2料煮開，續入麵炒拌均勻，放入3料翻拌即可。

■ 伊麵煮後口感鬆軟，有別於一般麵條的嚼勁。以上是最基本的伊麵做法，僅使用少量的配料。平常做時可隨意搭配肉類、海鮮或多種蔬菜於麵內。

BRAISED YEE-FU NOODLES

[SERVES 2]

1 {
1 t. shredded ginger root
2 black mushrooms
}

2 {
2 T. oyster sauce; ½ T. soy sauce
½ c. stock; dash of pepper
}

3 {
⅓ lb. (150g) total: bean sprouts, Chinese yellow chives
　　sections, shredded bell pepper
}

2 packages of dried Yee-fu noodles, 3½ oz (100g)

1 Soften mushrooms of 1 in cold water then shred. Mix 2 and set aside.

2 Boil enough water to cook noodles. When noodles become soft, remove and set them aside.

3 Heat 2 T. oil, stir-fry 1 until fragrant, add 2 and bring to a boil. Add noodles, and mix well. Add in 3; mix then serve.

■ Cooked Yee-Fu noodles have a soft, bouncy, and substantive texture unlike any other noodle. This recipe is the most basic method to prepare Yee-Fu Noodles since it calls for limited accompanying ingredients. Any kind of meat, seafood, or vegetable may be added to the noodles to create delicious varieties of this dish.

韭黃肉絲燴麵　NOODLES WITH PORK AND YELLOW CHIVES

【 廣東菜 】	【 2人份 】
瘦肉 (豬、牛或雞)...150公克(4兩)	
① 醬油、酒 、玉米粉...各2小匙	
② 香菇(泡軟切絲)...2朵	
洋蔥絲...1杯	
紅蘿蔔絲...½杯	
③ 水...1½杯	
醬油...1大匙	
鹽、糖...各½小匙	
胡椒...少許	
玉米粉...1½大匙	
④ 韭黃及其它蔬菜...(切段)共2杯	
乾麵...150公克(4兩)	

【 CANTONESE CUISINE 】	【 SERVES 2 】
⅓ lb. (150g) lean pork, beef or chicken	
① 2 t. ea.: soy sauce, cooking wine, cornstarch	
② 2 black mushrooms, softened in water and shredded	
1 c. shredded onions	
½ c. shredded carrot	
③ 1½ c. water; 1 T. soy sauce	
½ t. ea.: salt, sugar	
dash of pepper	
1½ T. cornstarch	
④ 2 c. total (cut in sections): Chinese yellow chives and other desired vegetables	
⅓ lb. (150g) dried noodles	

1　肉切絲加①料調勻，炒前拌入1大匙油則肉易炒散開。

2　油2大匙燒熱 ，先將肉絲炒開至熟撈出，再加油2大匙燒熱，依序放入②料炒香，續入③料燒開，攪拌成濃汁，放回肉絲再燒開後加入④料拌勻即離火。

3　多量水燒開，將麵放入滾水中，煮熟後撈起分盛在盤內，把煮好的料趁熱淋在麵上即成。

■　若欲事先煮麵，可將煮好的麵拌入½大匙的油，食前放入烤箱或微波爐內加熱，或煎兩面黃(見117頁)，再把煮好的料淋上。

1　Shred meat and mix with ①. Mix in 1 T. oil before stir-frying so meat will separate easily.

2　Heat 2 T. oil, then stir-fry meat until meat separates and is cooked; remove. Heat another 2 T. oil, add and stir-fry ② in the order listed, until fragrant. Add Mixture ③ and bring to a boil; stir to thicken. Add the cooked meat and heat until liquid bubbles; put in ④ and stir to mix well.

3　Boil enough water to cook noodles; when cooked, remove and divide into two serving dishes and top with the stir-fried mixture. Serve.

■　If the noodles are cooked in advance, mix the noodles with ½ T. oil to prevent them from sticking together. Heat the noodles in oven or microwave when ready to use. Precooked noodles may also be fried to make double-sided crispy noodles (p.117).

什錦兩面黃　DOUBLE-FACED GOLDEN NOODLES

1	蔥...6段
	薑片...6片
	蒜末...1小匙
2	雞肉、魷魚、叉燒肉...各6片
	蝦仁...6隻
3	青江菜...1棵
	筍片、紅蘿蔔片、香菇(泡軟) ...各6片
4	醬油、蠔油...各1大匙
	鹽...⅓小匙
	胡椒...少許
	高湯或水...1½杯
	麻油...½大匙
5	玉米粉...1½大匙
	水...2大匙
	細雞蛋麵...150公克 (4兩)

1　多量水燒開將麵條煮熟，撈出漂冷水瀝乾水份，攤開成圓餅狀備用。

2　油⅓杯燒熱，將麵餅(圖1)以中火煎炸3分鐘至兩面呈金黃色，煎時轉動鍋使麵餅均勻煎黃(圖2)，撈出置盤。

3　油3大匙燒熱，炒香1料，隨入2料炒1分鐘再加3料拌炒，續加4料燒開，以5料勾芡成濃稠狀，趁熱淋在麵餅上即成。

■　麵條煮熟後再煎炸過即為兩面黃，是廣東人傳統炒麵的手法之一，此道菜又稱 "廣州炒麵"。

1	6 pieces green onion
	6 ginger root slices
	1 t. minced garlic
2	6 slices ea.: chicken, squid, Cantonese BBQ pork
	6 shelled shrimp
3	1 stalk bok choy
	6 slices ea.: bamboo shoots, carrot, black mushrooms (softened in water and shredded)
4	1 T. ea.: soy sauce, oyster sauce
	⅓ t. salt
	dash of pepper
	1½ c. stock or water
	½ T. sesame oil
5	1½ T. cornstarch
	2 T. water
	⅓ lb. (150g) thin egg noodles

1　Boil enough water to cook noodles. When noodles are cooked, remove and immediately rinse in cold water and drain. Place the noodles on a plate and spread them to form a pancake shape.

2　Heat ⅓ c. oil and fry pancake shaped noodles (Fig. 1) for 3 minutes over medium heat until both sides turn a golden color. While cooking, move wok in a circular motion to ensure even cooking (Fig. 2). Remove noodles and put on a serving plate.

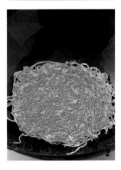

3　Heat 3 T. oil; stir-fry 1 until fragrant. Stir-fry 2 for 1 minute and add 3; mix well. Add 4 and bring to a boil. Add mixture 5 to thicken and immediately pour on noodles; serve.

■　After the noodles are cooked, they are pan-fried on both sides to yield "Double-faced Golden Noodles". This double-pan-frying technique is a traditional Cantonese method of preparing noodles. This dish is also known as "Guangzhou Fried Noodles".

番茄牛肉麵

【 2人份 】

牛肉片...150公克(4兩)

1 醬油、酒、玉米粉...各½大匙

2 蒜末...1大匙
洋蔥絲...1½杯
番茄塊...1杯

3 高湯或水...¾杯
醬油、番茄醬...各1大匙
糖...2小匙
玉米粉...1小匙
鹽、胡椒、麻油...各¼小匙

乾麵...150公克(4兩)

1 將牛肉加1料略醃。

2 多量水燒開，將麵條煮熟後撈出盛於兩盤。

3 油1大匙燒熱，將牛肉炒開至變色鏟出；再燒熱2大匙油，將2料依序放入炒香，加入3料燒開，最後加炒熟的牛肉燒開，淋在麵上，食時拌勻即可。也可將煮好的麵與湯料一起拌炒均勻後再盛盤。

NOODLES WITH BEEF AND TOMATOES

[SERVES 2]

⅓ lb. (150g) beef slices

1 ½ T. ea.: soy sauce, cooking wine, cornstarch

2 1 T. minced garlic
1½ c. shredded onions
1 c. tomato (cut into pieces)

3 ¾ c. stock or water
1 T. ea.: soy sauce, ketchup
2 t. sugar; 1 t. cornstarch
¼ t. ea.: salt, pepper, sesame oil

⅓ lb. (150g) dried noodles

1 Marinate beef in 1.

2 Boil enough water to cook noodles; when cooked, remove and place on two serving plates.

3 Heat 1 T. oil then stir-fry beef until meat separates and color changes; remove. Heat 2 T. oil; stir-fry 2 in the order listed until fragrant. Add 3 and bring to a boil; add cooked beef and bring to a boil. Pour the mixture on the noodles. Mix noodles and beef mixture well when serving. If desired, noodles and beef mixture may also be pre-mixed in the wok then served.

台式炒麵

【 2人份 】

1
- 油蔥酥、蝦米...各1大匙
- 韭菜白色部份...¼杯
- 香菇(泡軟切絲)...2朵
- 豬或雞肉絲...150公克(4兩)
- 辣豆瓣醬...½小匙
- 醬油...1大匙

2
- 水...½杯，醋...½大匙
- 鹽...¼小匙，胡椒...少許

3
- 豆芽菜...2杯
- 韭菜(切段)...1杯

台式油麵*...450公克(12兩)

1　多量水燒開，將麵川燙後撈出備用。

2　油2大匙燒熱，將①料依序放入炒香，加②料燒開，隨即入麵炒拌再加③料拌炒均勻即成。

■　傳統的台式炒麵或炒米粉主要是使用油蔥酥、韭菜（或蔥）、蝦米、香菇、肉等炒出獨特的香味，再加入煮熟的麵條或米粉炒拌，蔬菜可隨喜好搭配高麗菜或紅蘿蔔等。

TAIWANESE STYLE FRIED NOODLES

【 SERVES 2 】

1
- 1 T. ea.: fried shallots, dried shrimp
- ¼ c. white part of Chinese chives
- 2 black mushrooms, softened in water and shredded
- ⅛ lb. (150g) shredded pork or chicken
- ½ t. spicy bean paste; 1 T. soy sauce

2
- ½ c. water; ½ T. vinegar; ¼ t. salt
- dash of pepper

3
- 2 c. bean sprouts
- 1 c. Chinese chives sections

1 lb. (450g) cooked Taiwanese noodles

1　Blanch noodles in boiling water, drain and set aside.

2　Heat 2 T. oil; stir-fry ① in the order listed until fragrant. Add ② and bring to a boil, add the pre-cooked noodles. Add ③, stir-fry until mixed well. Serve.

■　Traditional Taiwanese fried noodles and fried rice vermicelli are made by stir-frying fried shallots or chives with dried shrimp, black mushrooms and meat to bring out the unique flavor, then mix in the cooked noodles or vermicelli. Different kinds of vegetables such as cabbage or carrots may be used as desired.

烏龍炒麵

肉絲(雞或豬)...150公克(4兩)

香菇(泡軟切絲)...2朶

① 洋蔥絲...½杯
　 高麗菜絲...2杯

② 水...½杯
　 醬油、烏醋...各1大匙
　 鹽、糖、麻油...各⅓小匙
　 胡椒...⅛小匙

辣椒粉...⅛小匙

熟烏龍麵*...450公克(12兩)

1　多量水燒開，將烏龍麵放入滾水中川燙後撈出。

2　油2大匙燒熱，先將香菇炒香，隨入肉絲炒開至變色，再依序入①料略炒後加②料燒開，放入烏龍麵炒拌均勻撒上辣椒粉即成。

*　若是買乾烏龍麵，則在多量水內煮到熟後撈出再使用。

STIR-FRIED UDON

[SERVES 2]

⅓ lb. (150g) shredded chicken or pork

2 black mushrooms, softened in water and shredded

① ½ c. shredded onions
　 2 c. shredded cabbage

② ½ c. water
　 1 T. ea.: soy sauce, black vinegar
　 ⅓ t. ea.: salt, sugar, sesame oil
　 ⅛ t. pepper

⅛ t. chili powder

1 lb. (450g) cooked Udon*

1　Blanch noodles in boiling water, drain and set aside.

2　Heat 2 T. oil; stir-fry mushrooms until fragrant. Add meat and stir-fry until meat is separated and color changes. Add in ① in the order listed, while briefly stir-frying. Add ② and bring to a boil; add the pre-cooked noodles and stir-fry to mix well. Sprinkle on chili powder and serve.

*　If dried udon is used, cook udon in boiling water until done. Drain udon then follow Step 2.

沙茶牛肉炒麵

【 2人份 】

1. 牛肉片...150公克 (4兩)
   醬油、酒、玉米粉...各½大匙
   空心菜(略切)...225公克 (6兩)

2. 蔥、薑、蒜末...各½大匙
   沙茶醬...1½大匙
   醬油...1大匙

3. 水...¾杯，糖...½小匙
   鹽...½小匙，胡椒...少許
   乾麵...150公克(4兩)

1 牛肉片加1料拌醃備用。

2 多量水燒開，將麵條煮熟後撈出，加1大匙油略拌以免麵條黏在一起。

3 油1大匙燒熱，先入空心菜再加1大匙水略炒盛出，擦乾鍋面。

4 油3大匙燒熱，將肉炒開至熟鏟出，用餘油將2料依序放入炒香，隨入3料燒開，最後加麵、牛肉及空心菜一同炒勻即可。

SA-TSA BBQ BEEF WITH NOODLES

[SERVES 2]

⅓ lb. (150g) beef slices
1. ½ T. ea.: soy sauce, cooking wine, cornstarch
   ½ lb. (225g) water spinach, roughly cut

2. ½ T. ea.(minced): green onion, ginger root, garlic
   1½ T. sa-tsa BBQ paste
   1 T. soy sauce

3. ¾ c. water
   ½ t. ea.: sugar, salt
   dash of pepper
   ⅓ lb. (150g) dried noodles

1 Marinate beef in 1, set aside.

2 Boil enough water to cook noodles; when noodles are cooked, remove and add 1 T. oil so noodles will not stick together.

3 Heat 1 T. oil; add water spinach then 1 T. water, stir-fry briefly and remove. Wipe wok dry.

4 Heat 3 T. oil and stir-fry beef until meat separates and is cooked; remove the meat. With remaining oil, stir-fry 2 in the order listed until fragrant. Add 3 and bring to boil, add cooked noodles, beef and spinach; stir-fry to mix well.

蝦仁炒麵

【 2人份 】

蝦仁...150公克(4兩)

① 鹽...¼小匙，玉米粉、酒...各1大匙

蛋...2個

② 蒜末...½大匙，洋蔥片、甜椒片...共½杯

③ 醬油、烏醋...各1大匙
糖、鹽、麻油...各1小匙

菠菜...225公克(6兩)，乾麵...150公克(4兩)

1 蝦仁去腸泥洗淨瀝乾以①料略醃；多量水燒開，
將麵條煮熟後撈出，拌入1大匙油；菠菜川燙後漂
冷水瀝乾；蛋打散備用。

2 油1大匙燒熱，放入蛋液炒至凝固鏟出。再用1大
匙油將蝦炒熟至變色鏟出。

3 油1大匙燒熱，炒香②料，隨入③料、麵、菠菜、
蛋和蝦，炒拌均勻即可。

■ 這道麵是乾炒的，故③料內不加水；雞蛋可用肉
絲或肉片取代。

FRIED NOODLES WITH GARLIC SHRIMP

【 SERVES 2 】

⅓ lb. (150g) shelled shrimp

① ¼ t. salt
1 T. ea.: cornstarch, cooking wine

2 eggs

② ½ T. minced garlic
½ c. total(sliced): onions, bell peppers

③ 1 T. ea.: soy sauce, black vinegar
1 t. ea.: sugar, salt, sesame oil

½ lb. (225g) spinach

⅓ lb. (150g) dried noodles

1 Devein shrimp, wash and drain. Pat dry and marinate
in ①. Boil enough water to cook noodles, when
cooked remove and mix in 1 T. oil so noodles do
not stick together. Blanch spinach and immediately
immerse in cold water and drain. Beat eggs and
set aside.

2 Heat 1 T. oil; stir-fry eggs until firm; remove. Heat
1 T. oil and stir-fry shrimp until cooked and color
changes; remove.

3 Heat 1 T. oil; stir-fry ② until fragrant, add ③, cooked
noodles, spinach, eggs and shrimp; stir-fry to mix
well.

■ This dish tastes best when fried dry without liquid;
therefore, do not add water into ③. Shredded or
sliced meat may be used instead of eggs.

台式炒米粉

【 2人份 】

① 油蔥酥...1大匙，蝦米...2大匙，香菇(切絲)...2朵
　　瘦肉絲(豬或雞)...150公克(4兩)
　　醬油...1大匙

② 洋蔥絲...1杯，包心菜絲...2杯，紅蘿蔔絲...½杯

③ 水...¾杯，鹽...½小匙，胡椒...少許
　　乾米粉...150公克(4兩)

1 乾米粉用冷水泡5分鐘撈出備用。

2 油4大匙燒熱，依序放入①料炒香，再加醬油及②料略炒，隨入③料燒開，放入米粉翻拌至汁收乾，可隨喜好加香菜，適與辣椒醬配食。

■ 泡過水的米粉炒前可先用微波爐加熱2分鐘，再與全部材料翻拌，可縮短炒米粉的時間。

TAIWANESE STYLE RICE VERMICELLI

[SERVES 2]

① 1 T. fried shallots; 2 T. dried shrimp
　2 black mushrooms, softened in water and shredded
　⅓ lb. (150g) shredded lean pork or chicken
　1 T. soy sauce

② 1 c. shredded onions
　2 c. shredded cabbage
　½ c. shredded carrots

③ ¾ c. water
　½ t. salt
　dash of pepper
　⅓ lb. (150g) dried rice vermicelli

1 Soak rice vermicelli in cold water for five minutes; remove and set aside.

2 Heat 4 T. oil; add and stir-fry ① in the order listed until fragrant. Add soy sauce and ② and stir-fry briefly. Add ③ and bring to a boil; add rice vermicelli and stir-fry until all liquid is evaporated. Cilantro may be added as desired. Best served with chili paste.

■ After soaking the vermicelli in cold water, cooking at high for two minutes in a microwave oven can shorten the time of stir-frying.

星洲炒米粉

【 2人份 】

1. 叉燒肉絲*、魷魚絲...各½杯
   蝦仁...8隻

2. 筍絲、包心菜絲...共1杯
   紅蘿蔔絲...½杯
   豆芽菜...2杯

3. 蒜末、蝦米...各1大匙
   洋蔥絲...1杯

   咖哩粉...1大匙

4. 高湯或水...1杯
   鹽、糖...各2小匙
   胡椒...⅛小匙，麻油...1大匙

   乾米粉...150公克(4兩)

1. 將米粉用沸水泡1分鐘撈出，再用冷水泡3分鐘撈出瀝乾水份。

2. 油3大匙燒熱，放入①料炒1分鐘，再加②料炒2分鐘，取出備用。

3. 油2大匙燒熱，先炒香③料，隨入咖哩粉略拌，再加④料及米粉炒1分鐘，續入炒好的①料及②料翻炒均勻即成。

* 叉燒肉做法詳見145頁，若無叉燒肉絲可以一般肉絲取代。

SINGAPOREAN CURRY RICE VERMICELLI

【 SERVES 2 】

1. ½ c. ea.(shredded): B.B.Q. pork*, squid
   8 shelled shrimp

2. 1 c. total (shredded): bamboo shoots, cabbage
   ½ c. shredded carrots
   2 c. bean sprouts

3. 1 T. ea.: minced garlic, dried shrimp
   1 c. shredded onions

   1 T. curry powder

4. 1 c. stock or water
   2 t. ea.: salt, sugar
   ⅛ t. pepper; 1 T. sesame oil

   ⅓ lb. (150g) dried rice vermicelli

1 Soak rice vermicelli in boiling water for one minute; remove then soak in cold water for three minutes. Remove and drain.

2 Heat 3 T. oil; stir-fry ① for one minute. Add ② and stir-fry for two minutes; remove.

3 Heat 2 T. oil; stir-fry ③ until fragrant. Add curry powder and stir briefly; add ④ and rice vermicelli, stir-fry one minute. Return ① and ② to the wok, mix well and serve.

* To make B.B.Q pork, see p.145. Shredded cooked beef or chicken may be used instead of B.B.Q. pork.

干炒牛河

【 廣東菜 】

【 2人份 】

牛肉片...150公克(4兩)

1 醬油、酒...各½大匙
  玉米粉...½大匙

2 生抽...2大匙，老抽...1大匙
  麻油...½小匙，胡椒...少許

3 豆芽菜、洋蔥絲、紅蘿蔔絲、
  蔥段...共225公克(6兩)

河粉...450公克(12兩)

1 將河粉一片一片分開；牛肉加
  1料略醃。

2 油1大匙燒熱，將肉炒開至變
  色撈出。

3 油2大匙燒熱，將河粉放入炒
  開，等炒熱後加入調勻的2料
  及牛肉炒拌均勻，最後拌入3
  料略炒即可。

■ 河粉冷藏之後不易分開，故購
  買後若有需要放入冰箱，需先
  將河粉分開之後才冷藏。炒河
  粉時宜使用不粘鍋，以免河粉
  粘鍋；因不加鹽，故炒河粉的
  調味完全靠生抽及老抽，若味
  道太淡，生抽及老抽可以2：1
  的比例增加。

SAUTEED BEEF WITH RICE NOODLES

[CANTONESE CUISINE]

[SERVES 2]

⅓ lb. (150g) sliced beef

1 ½ T. ea.: soy sauce, cooking wine
   ½ T. cornstarch

2 2 T. light soy sauce (sen cho)
   1 T. dark soy sauce (lao cho)
   ½ t. sesame oil
   dash of pepper

3 ½ lb. (225g) total: bean spouts, shredded onions, carrots
   and green onions

1 lb. (450g) fresh rice noodles

1 Separate the rice noodles to keep them from sticking to each other. Set aside. Mix beef with 1.

2 Heat 1 T. oil; stir-fry meat until separated and meat changes color. Remove the meat and set aside.

3 Heat 2 T. oil; stir-fry noodles until separated and hot. Add mixture 2 and beef; stir-fry to mix well, add 3 and briefly stir-fry. Serve.

■ If fresh noodles are kept in a refrigerator for later use, separate the noodles before refrigerating. Using a non-stick pan to fry rice noodles can prevent the noodles from sticking to the pan. Salt is not used in this dish; the taste of this dish comes from the soy sauce. If a stronger taste is preferred, increase the amount of light and dark soy sauce at the ratio of 2:1.

炒年糕

【 2人份 】

瘦肉片(牛、豬或雞)
...150公克(4兩)

1 [醬油、酒、玉米粉...各½大匙

2 [蔥...8段，香菇(切絲)...2朵
蝦米...2大匙

醬油...1大匙

3 [水...¼杯，鹽...⅛小匙
胡椒...隨意

4 [小白菜(略切)、紅蘿蔔片
...共225公克(6兩)

年糕片...225 公克(6兩)

1 冷藏的年糕片泡水2小時後撈
出備用。

2 肉加1料拌勻，炒前再拌入1大
匙油則易炒散。

3 油3大匙燒熱，將2料依序放入
炒香再入肉片炒開至變色，隨
入醬油、3料及年糕片略炒，
再加4料炒拌，若火力小則蓋
鍋燜1分鐘，見蔬菜微軟年糕熟
透即可，食時可加辣豆瓣醬。

■ 年糕需炒至熟透，但不宜太軟
爛，要有Q的口感才好吃。

STIR-FRIED RICE CAKE

【 SERVES 2 】

⅓ lb. (150g) sliced lean beef, pork or chicken

1 [½ T. ea.: soy sauce, cooking wine, cornstarch

2 [8 pieces green onion
2 T. dried shrimp
2 black mushrooms, softened in water and sliced

1 T. soy sauce

3 [¼ c. water; ⅛ t. salt
dash of pepper

4 [½ lb. (225g) total: short bok choy (roughly cut), sliced carrot

½ lb. (225g) rice cake slices

1 Take rice cake slices from refrigerator and soak in water for two hours. Remove and set aside.

2 Mix meat with 1; mix 1 T. oil before stir-frying so slices will separate easily.

3 Heat 3 T. oil; add and stir-fry 2 in the order listed until fragrant. Stir-fry meat until separated and color changes. Add soy sauce, 3 and rice cakes. Briefly stir-fry and add 4. If not enough heat, cover and cook for one minute until vegetables and rice cakes are completely cooked. Serve with hot bean paste if desired.

■ Rice cake needs to be cooked thoroughly, but do not overcook to retain chewy texture.

木須肉包餅

【 6個 】

瘦肉絲(豬、牛或雞)
150公克...(4兩)

1
醬油、酒...各1小匙
玉米粉...½大匙

蛋(打散)...2個

菠菜(切段)...150公克(4兩)

2
蔥絲、薑絲...共2大匙
香菇絲、木耳絲、筍絲...共¾杯

3
醬油、酒...各½大匙
鹽、糖、麻油...各¼小匙

荷葉餅...6張，海鮮醬...3大匙

1 肉絲調入1料略醃。

2 油1大匙燒熱，倒入蛋液炒至凝固鏟出；另用一大匙油將菠菜略炒撈出，湯汁不要。

3 油2大匙燒熱，依序放入2料炒香，隨入肉炒開至變色，再加蛋、菠菜及3料拌炒均勻鏟出。

4 每張荷葉餅內隨意塗抹海鮮醬，將炒好的木須肉放入6張餅內捲成春捲狀食用。

MU-SHU PORK WITH LOTUS CREPES

【 MAKES 6 】

⅓ lb. (150g) shredded pork, beef, or chicken

1
1 t. ea.: soy sauce, cooking wine
½ T. cornstarch

2 eggs (slightly beaten)

⅓ lb. (150g) spinach, cut into pieces

2
2 T. total (shredded): green onion, ginger root
¾ c. total (shredded) : black mushrooms, black wood ears, bamboo shoots

3
½ T. ea.: soy sauce, cooking wine
¼ t. ea.: salt, sugar, sesame oil

6 lotus crepes*;   3 T. hoisin sauce

1 Marinate meat in 1.

2 Heat 1 T. oil; stir-fry eggs until firm, remove. Heat 1 T. oil; stir-fry spinach briefly and remove. Discard liquid.

3 Heat 2 T. oil; add and stir-fry 2 in the order listed until fragrant. Add meat and stir-fry until meat separates and color changes. Add eggs, spinach and 3, stir-fry to mix well. Remove.

4 Spread hoisin sauce on each crepe, top with stir-fried mixture and roll up like an egg roll. Serve.

* Lotus crepes are made of all-purpose flour and are available at some Chinese supermarkets. If unavailable, flour tortillas may be used.

蚵仔麵線

【 台灣菜 】

【 2人份 】

蚵...225公克(6兩)
薑末、酒...各1小匙
玉米粉...1小匙
1 ⎡ 蒜頭(拍扁)...2瓣，蝦米...1大匙
⎣ 醬油...1大匙
2 ⎡ 罐頭雞湯...2杯，水...3杯
⎣ 胡椒...¼小匙
九層塔或香菜...1杯
3 ⎡ 玉米粉、水...各3大匙
4 ⎡ 烏醋、辣椒醬、油蔥酥、蒜泥
⎣ ...隨意
白麵線*...115公克(3兩)

1　薑末加酒後再擠出汁，此為薑酒汁，用來除去腥味。

2　蚵加鹽2小匙、水2大匙輕抓後洗數次，放入開水内川燙，撈出瀝乾水份，加薑酒汁與玉米粉拌勻備用。

3　油2大匙燒熱，炒香1料，加醬油及2料燒開，放入麵線再燒開，續入蚵及九層塔燒開，以調勻的3料勾茨成濃稠狀，酌量加4料調味，趁熱食用。

*　傳統路邊攤的蚵仔麵線使用紅麵線，因為這種麵線比白麵線耐煮，適合煮好一大鍋後再推到市場販賣。紅色或白色麵線口感不同，可自行選擇。有的麵線本身很鹹，宜先用大量滾水漂煮去除部分鹹味之後再使用。

OYSTER SOUP WITH THIN NOODLES

【 TAIWANESE CUISINE 】

【 SERVES 2 】

½ lb. (225g) oysters
1 t. ea.: minced ginger root, cooking wine
1 t. cornstarch
1 ⎡ 2 garlic cloves, smashed; 1 T. dried shrimp
⎣ 1 T. soy sauce
2 ⎡ 2 c. canned chicken broth; 3 c. water; ¼ t. pepper
1 c. basil or cilantro
3 ⎡ 3 T. ea.: cornstarch, water
4 ⎡ black vinegar, chili paste, fried shallots, or ground garlic as desired
¼ lb. (115g) thin noodles*

1　Mix ginger and wine to make ginger wine. Set aside.

2　Mix 2 t. salt and 2 T. water with oysters; rinse several times. Blanch oysters in boiling water, remove and drain. Combine oysters with ginger wine and cornstarch.

3　Heat 2 T. oil; stir-fry 1 until fragrant, add soy sauce and 2, bring to a boil. Add the noodles and boil again. Add oysters and basil, boil again. Add mixture 3 to thicken. Season with 4 and serve.

*　Traditionally sold by street vendors, the thin noodles used in this dish are the brown-colored variety that retain a firm consistency. This unique firmness enables the vendors to prepare a large pot ahead of time and then transport the noodles to their stands. The thin noodles come in white or brown, and each has a different consistency, readers may choose according to availability. Some brands of thin noodles can be very salty; it is best to boil them in a lot of water to reduce their saltiness before use.

麻油雞麵線

【 4人份 】

雞...900公克(1½斤)，老薑...1塊

黑麻油...4大匙，酒...4杯

① 水(或酒)...2杯，糖...1小匙

　　當歸(無亦可)...1片

白麵線...300公克(8兩)

1　雞切塊，老薑不去皮切出12大薄片。

2　將麻油與薑片放入鍋內，以中火爆香3分鐘呈金黃色，推至一邊，改大火將雞塊煎炒5分鐘呈微黃，再把薑片推入，加酒燒開以中火煮約10分鐘後，再加①料續煮15至20分鐘或視個人喜好雞肉熟度。將煮好的麻油雞分裝在4個碗內。

3　多量水燒開，放入麵線煮約1分鐘至麵熟，立即撈出分放4碗麻油雞湯內。

■　若將麵線放入麻油湯內，大部分湯汁會被麵線吸收。喜愛喝湯者可先舀出少許浮油及湯汁拌入麵線內，另外再盛一碗麻油雞湯配食，如此不僅能讓麵線口感Q，且喝得出雞湯的香濃味。麻油雞是婦女坐月子時的養生補品，通常不加鹽，加當歸主要是取其香味。

SESAME FLAVORED CHICKEN SOMEN

[SERVES 4]

2 lbs. (900g) chicken; 1 ginger root

4 T. black sesame oil; 4 c. rice wine

① **2 c. water or rice wine; 1 t. sugar**

1 piece of Dang-Kuei (optional)

⅔ lb. (300g) somen (thin noodles)

1　Cut chicken into pieces. Slice twelve large pieces of ginger root, do not remove skin.

2　Cook sesame oil and ginger for three minutes over medium heat until fragrant and color becomes golden; move ginger to the side. Add chicken and stir-fry over high heat for five minutes until cooked and color changes; return ginger and add wine, bring to a boil. Cook ten minutes over medium heat, add ① and cook 15 or 20 minutes to get desired texture. Remove and put the sesame chicken soup into four large soup bowls.

3　Boil enough water to immerse somen and cook for one minute until done. Remove and divide the somen to the four soup bowls.

■　If somen are put into the sesame chicken soup, they will absorb all the soup. For those who enjoy drinking the soup, put the noodles in a separate bowl and add a little bit of the soup and the grease. Serving the aromatic chicken soup in another bowl allows full appreciation of the flavor of the soup as well as retaining the texture of the noodles. "Sesame Chicken Soup" is an especially fortifying, nutritious soup to which salt is usually not added and served to mothers after childbirth. The dang-guey's main effect is to add its unique medicinal benefits and aromatic fragrance to the soup.

米 麵 小菜

CHINESE RICE

NOODLES **APPETIZERS**

簡餐 SOUPS

SWEETS 湯

甜點

雞絲沙拉

【 4人份 】

帶骨雞胸或雞腿...450公克(12兩)

餛飩皮(切絲)...12張

① 生菜絲...3½杯
洋蔥絲、紅蘿蔔絲...共½杯
小黃瓜絲...1杯

② 鹽...½小匙
醋...1½大匙
糖...1小匙
醬油、麻油...各1大匙
胡椒...少許

炒熟白芝麻...1大匙

1 水燒開，放入雞胸(水蓋過雞即可)，煮約25分鐘(中途需翻面)至熟取出，待涼後去骨，肉撕成絲或切粗條；將②料調在碗內；餛飩皮炸酥備用。

2 食時將雞肉絲、①料、②料及餛飩皮絲拌勻，上撒白芝麻即成。

■ 沙拉內若不放炸餛飩皮，則②料內須多加油3大匙。如無白芝麻亦可改用碎花生。

CHINESE CHICKEN SALAD

【 SERVES 4 】

1 lb. (450g) chicken breast or legs (with bone)

12 won ton skins, shredded

① **3½ c. shredded lettuce**
½ c. total (shredded): onions, carrot
1 c. Japanese or gherkin cucumber, shredded

② **½ t. salt; 1½ T. vinegar; 1 t. sugar**
1 T. ea.: soy sauce, sesame oil
dash of pepper

1 T. roasted white sesame seeds

1 Boil just enough water to cover the chicken; immerse chicken and cook for twenty-five minutes or until cooked, turn chicken over during cooking. Remove and let cool. Separate meat from bones, tear into shreds or cut into strips. Mix ② in a bowl and set aside. Fry won ton shreds until golden, set aside.

2 Mix shredded chicken with ①, ②, and won ton shreds. Sprinkle sesame seeds on top and serve.

■ If crispy won ton shreds are not added to the salad, add 3 T. oil to ②. Crushed peanuts may be used instead of white sesame seeds.

番茄黃瓜沙拉　TOMATO CUCUMBER SALAD

【 4人份 】

番茄、小黃瓜...共300公克(8兩)

① 鹽、糖...各⅓小匙，醋或檸檬汁...⅔大匙
油及麻油...共2大匙，胡椒...隨意

1　番茄、小黃瓜切塊(共兩杯)，加入①料拌勻，
　　現拌現食。

■　除番茄、黃瓜外可加入一些當季盛產的水果，
　　例如橘子、蘋果或鳳梨等。

【 SERVES 4 】

⅔ lb. (300g) tomatoes, Japanese or gherkin
　　cucumbers

⅓ t. ea.: salt, sugar

① ⅔ T. vinegar or lemon juice

2 T. total: oil, sesame oil

pepper as desired

1　Cut tomatoes and cucumbers into pieces to
　　total two cups. Add ① and mix well; serve.

■　Seasonal fruit such as oranges, apples or
　　pineapple may be used instead of tomatoes
　　and cucumbers to make the salad.

酸辣黃瓜　SPICY TANGY CUCUMBERS

【 4人份 】

小黃瓜... 300公克(8兩)

① 糖、麻油...各1大匙，醋...3大匙
辣豆瓣醬...2大匙，蒜末...½大匙

1　小黃瓜洗淨切去頭尾，切3公分長段後拍裂開成3
　　至4塊，加鹽⅔小匙醃20分鐘後，再沖洗去鹽水
　　後擠乾。

2　將①料加入小黃瓜中拌勻，置冰箱冷藏並隨時翻
　　拌以便入味，醃1小時之後即可享用或置冰箱數
　　天分次食用。

【 SERVES 4 】

⅔ lb. (300g) Japanese or gherkin cucumbers

3 T. vinegar; 1 T. ea.: sugar, sesame oil

① 2 T. spicy bean paste; ½ T. minced garlic

1　Wash cucumbers, slice off both ends and discard.
　　Cut cucumbers into 1¼"(3 cm) long pieces.
　　Smash each piece to become three or four pieces.
　　Add ⅔ t. salt and marinate twenty minutes.
　　Wash off salt and squeeze out water.

2　Mix cucumbers with ①; put in refrigerator for one
　　hour, stir occasionally to absorb flavor. Marinated
　　cucumbers can be kept fresh in the refrigerator
　　for several days. May be divided into small por-
　　tions for later use.

涼拌高麗菜　CABBAGE SALAD

【 4人份 】

高麗菜...300公克(8兩)

1 鹽...⅓小匙，糖...1小匙

醋、麻油...各1大匙

1 高麗菜洗淨切絲(約4杯)，加入①料拌勻食用，
現拌現食。

■ 可任選香菜、蒜、紅辣椒、洋蔥或小黃瓜與高
麗菜一起搭配。

涼拌青花菜 青花菜燙熟後漂冷水，瀝乾水份
再拌入①料即可。

【 SERVES 4 】

⅔ lb. (300g) cabbage

1 ⅓ t. salt;　1 t. sugar

1 T. ea.: vinegar, sesame oil

1 Wash cabbage and shred to get 4 cups. Add
①; mix and serve immediately.

■ Shredded cilantro, red chili peppers, onions,
gherkin cucumber or garlic cloves may be
added to the cabbage salad.

BROCCOLI SALAD Cook broccoli, blanch in cold
water, drain then mix with ①.

涼拌白蘿蔔　WHITE RADISH SALAD

【 4人份 】

白蘿蔔...300公克(8兩)

1 鹽...¼小匙，糖、醋、麻油...各1大匙

2 蒜末、紅辣椒絲...各1小匙，香菜末...隨意

1 白蘿蔔切薄片，加鹽⅔小匙醃約10分鐘至軟，
再沖洗去鹽份後擠乾，加上①料及②料混合拌
勻，可即食或置冰箱數天分次食用。

■ 可隨意拌入檸檬皮絲或紫蘇絲，味道更清香。

【 SERVES 4 】

⅔ lb. (300g) white radish

1 ¼ t. salt

1 T. ea.: sugar, vinegar, sesame oil

2 1 t. minced garlic

1 t. shredded red chili pepper

chopped cilantro as desired

1 Slice radish into thin slices, marinate in ⅔ t. salt
for 10 minutes until radish softens. Rinse to
remove salt; squeeze out excess water. Add ①
and ②; mix well. May save in refrigerator for
several days, or serve immediately.

■ Shredded lemon zest may be added for extra
flavor.

涼拌甜豆　SWEET PEA SALAD

【 4人份 】

甜豆...300公克(8兩)

[1] 鹽...¼小匙，麻油...1大匙

1　甜豆摘去筋，洗淨備用。

2　水燒開，將甜豆放入滾水內川燙，取出沖冷水
　　瀝乾，拌入[1]料即可。

■　可用豌豆夾、芹菜或其他蔬菜取代甜豆。若喜
　　歡熱食則不需沖冷水，燙熟後拌入[1]料即可。

【 SERVES 4 】

⅔ lb. (300g) sweet peas

[1] ¼ t. salt

1 T. sesame oil

1　Remove strings from sweet peas; wash and set
　　aside.

2　Boil water and blanch sweet peas, remove and
　　immediately rinse in cold water. Drain and mix in
　　[1]. Serve.

■　Chinese pea pods, celery or other vegetables
　　may be used instead of sweet peas. To serve
　　hot, do not rinse vegetables in cold water and
　　mix in [1] immediately after blanching.

廣東泡菜　CANTONESE PICKLED SALAD

【 4人份 】

[1] 白蘿蔔、紅蘿蔔、小黃瓜...切塊共4杯(1斤，600公克)
紅辣椒...1支，嫩薑...20片

[2] 醋、糖...各3大匙

1　將[1]料用鹽2小匙醃3小時後沖洗擠乾，加[2]料浸
　　泡3小時以上即可，若置冰箱可保存3、4天。

■　小黃瓜需先去籽再切塊，泡菜醃漬時間要夠長
　　才能入味，內加紅辣椒及薑是為增加泡菜的味
　　道，也可不加。

【 SERVES 4 】

4 c. (1⅓ lbs, 600g) total(cut in pieces):

[1] white radish, carrot, gherkin cucumber

1 red chili pepper;　20 slices baby ginger root

[2] 3 T. ea.: vinegar, sugar

1　Marinate [1] in 2 t. salt for 3 hours. Rinse to
　　remove salt and squeeze out excess water. Add
　　[2] and soak for more than three hours and up to
　　four days in the refrigerator. May serve anytime
　　during this period.

■　Remove cucumber seeds before cutting into
　　pieces.　Vegetables need to be marinated for a
　　sufficient time for optimal flavor.　Red chili pepper
　　and ginger root may be added for extra flavor.

涼拌苦瓜 | BITTER MELON SALAD

【 4人份 】

苦瓜(去籽及白肉)...300公克(8兩)

[1] 淡色醬油...2大匙

炒熟白芝麻、柴魚片...各2大匙

1 苦瓜切片，用沸水燙1分鐘或用微波爐加熱約2分鐘，立即浸泡冰水至涼透，瀝乾水份，依序加入[1]料拌勻即可。

■ 冰透的苦瓜亦可沾沙拉醬食用。

【 SERVES 4 】

⅔ lb (300g) bitter melon, seeds removed

[1] 2 T. light soy sauce

2 T. roasted white sesame seeds

2 T. bonito shavings

1 Slice melon into thin slices. Blanch in boiling water for 1 minute, or microwave at high for 2 minutes. Immerse in ice water immediately until cold, remove and drain. Add [1] in the order listed; mix well and serve.

■ Cold bitter melon salad may be served with mayonnaise without using [1].

涼拌西芹 | CELERY SALAD

【 4人份 】

芹菜...300公克(8兩)

[1] 鹽...¼小匙，糖、醋...各1小匙，芥末醬...2小匙

1 將[1]料拌勻備用。

2 芹菜略去老筋，洗淨切條狀，放入滾水內川燙1分鐘或用微波爐加熱約2分鐘，取出沖冷水並瀝乾，拌入[1]料後置冰箱冰涼即可。

■ 調勻的[1]料也可用來拌黃瓜、苦瓜片或高麗菜絲等其他蔬菜。

【 SERVES 4 】

⅔ lb. (300g) celery

[1] ¼ t. salt; 2 t. mustard

1 t. ea.: sugar, vinegar

1 Mix [1] and set aside.

2 Remove celery strings. Wash and cut into pieces; blanch in boiling water for 1 minute, or microwave at high for 2 minutes. Rinse in cold water and drain. Mix in [1], then refrigerate. Serve cold.

■ Mixture [1] may be used to mix other vegetables such as cucumber pieces, sliced bitter melon, and shredded cabbage.

涼拌芝麻菠菜　SPINACH SALAD WITH SESAME

菠菜...300公克(8兩)

1 ┌ 鹽...¼小匙，麻油...1大匙
  └ 炒熟白芝麻...1小匙，柴魚片...隨意

1　菠菜洗淨切段，入滾水內川燙約1分鐘或用微波爐加熱約2分鐘立即漂冷水，擠乾水份。

2　將燙熟的菠菜拌入1料，上撒白芝麻及柴魚片即可。

⅔ lb. (300g) spinach

1 ┌ ¼ t. salt
  │ 1 T. sesame oil
  │ 1 t. roasted white sesame seeds
  └ bonito shavings as desired

1　Cut spinach into pieces and blanch in boiling water for 1 minute, or cook in a microwave at high for 2 minutes. Immediately immerse in cold water, drain and squeeze out excess water.

2　Mix 1 with spinach, sprinkle on sesame seeds and bonito shavings.

涼拌海帶絲　TOSSED SEAWEED SALAD

海帶絲*...300公克(8兩)

1 ┌ 薑絲、蔥絲...各1大匙，蒜、紅辣椒末...各½大匙
2 └ 麻油、醬油...各2大匙，鹽...⅓小匙，醋...1大匙

1　海帶絲洗淨切段，放入滾水中煮開即撈出瀝乾拌入1料、2料，混合拌勻即可食用。

*　若使用乾海帶絲，泡水時需經常換水以去除粘液。56公克的乾海帶絲泡水1小時後可得約300公克(4杯)。

⅔ lb. (300g) shredded seaweed*

1 ┌ 1 T. ea. (shredded): ginger root, green onion
  └ ½ T. ea (minced): garlic, red chili pepper
2 ┌ 2 T. ea.: sesame oil, soy sauce
  └ ⅓ t. salt; 1 T. vinegar

1　Cut seaweed into pieces, place in boiling water and remove when water boils again. Drain seaweed. Mix with 1 and 2; serve.

*　If dried seaweed is used, soak in water until soft, change water several times to remove sticky membrane. 2 oz (56g) dried seaweed yields ⅔ lbs (300g) or 4 cups of seaweed when soaked 1 hour.

辣味毛豆 | SPICY SOYBEANS

【 4人份 】

冷凍毛豆莢...300公克(8兩)

① 紅辣椒(略切)...½支，蒜末、麻油...各2大匙
鹽...½小匙，胡椒...隨意

1 將冷凍毛豆莢放入滾水中川燙或用微波爐加熱約2分鐘，拌入①料即可。

■ 將八角與水煮出香味之後再放入毛豆莢燙煮，撈出與①料拌勻，即能做出八角風味的辣味毛豆。①料內的紅辣椒可用辣豆瓣醬取代。

【 SERVES 4 】

⅔ lb. (300g) frozen soybeans

① ½ red chili pepper, cut into pieces
2 T. ea.: minced garlic, sesame oil
½ t. salt; pepper as desired

1 Blanch soybeans in boiling water, or cook in microwave at high for 2 minutes. Mix with ① and serve.

■ Cook star Anise with water until fragrant, add soybeans and follow the above procedure ① to make unique flavored spicy soybeans. Chili bean paste may be used instead of red chili pepper in ①.

蒜泥茄子 | EGGPLANT SALAD WITH GARLIC SAUCE

【 4人份 】

長茄子...300公克(8兩)

① 醬油、蒜泥...各2大匙
麻油...1大匙，糖、醋...各1小匙

1 將①料拌勻；茄子去頭尾，洗淨切段。

2 水燒開，放入茄子煮約5分鐘，煮至茄子表面略為起皺能用筷子插透即取出待涼。

3 將茄子撕成條狀，置盤後酌量淋上①料即成。

■ 上述①料可做為不同蔬菜或肉類的淋汁。

【 SERVES 4 】

⅔ lb. (300g) Asian eggplants

① 2 T. ea.: soy sauce, ground garlic
1 T. sesame oil
1 t. ea.: sugar, vinegar

1 Mix ①; cut off ends of eggplants and then cut into pieces and set aside.

2 Cook eggplant in boiling water for 5 minutes until skin wrinkles and can be penetrated by a chopstick. Remove and let cool.

3 Tear eggplant into strips and place on a plate, pour desired amount of ① on top of eggplant. Serve.

■ May use ① on meat or other desired vegetables.

五味海鮮

魷魚...300公克(8兩)	
①	番茄醬...2大匙
	醬油、黑醋、麻油...各1大匙
	糖...½大匙
	蔥、薑末...各1小匙
	蒜、紅辣椒末...各1小匙

1　魷魚去皮洗淨，在內面切交叉花紋(見P.101頁)再切塊。

2　魷魚入滾水中川燙1分鐘至捲起即撈出，迅速沖冷水後瀝乾，食時沾或淋上調勻的①料即可。

■　章魚、乾魷魚(圖1)、新鮮干貝皆可用此方式料理。乾魷魚使用前需先泡發。

FIVE FLAVORED SEAFOOD COCKTAIL

⅔ lb. (300g): squid	
①	2 T. ketchup
	1 T. ea.: soy sauce, black vinegar, sesame oil
	½ T. sugar
	1 t. ea.(minced): green onion, ginger root, garlic,
	red chili pepper

1　Peel off the membrane of the squid; rinse and drain. Make diagonal cuts ⅔ deep on inside surface of the squid; turn and make diagonal cuts ⅔ deep to form crisscross cuts (p.101), and then cut into pieces.

2　Cook squid in boiling water for one minute until it curls; immediately remove and rinse in cold water then drain. When serving, dip in mixed ①, or pour mixed ① on top of the seafood.

■　Octopus, dried squid (Fig. 1), or fresh scallops may be used to make this cold dish. Dried squid should be soaked in water until expanded before use.

皮蛋豆腐 | TOFU WITH THOUSAND-YEAR-OLD EGGS

【 4人份 】

皮蛋(圖1)...2個，豆腐...300公克(8兩)

1 [醬油膏...2大匙，麻油...1大匙

蔥花或香菜末...1大匙

1 將皮蛋去殼與豆腐分別切塊盛盤，酌量淋上 1 料，撒上蔥花或香菜末即成。

■ 可隨喜好加肉鬆、柴魚片或醃過的嫩薑搭配食用，別具風味。

【 SERVES 4 】

2 preserved eggs (Fig. 1)

⅔ lb. (300g) tofu, regular

1 [**2 T. soy paste**

1 T. sesame oil

1 T. chopped green onion or minced cilantro

1 Shell the eggs. Cut eggs and tofu into pieces and place on a plate. Pour on desired amount of 1, sprinkle on onions or cilantro and serve.

■ Ground fried pork, bonito shavings, or marinated slices of baby ginger root may be added for extra flavor.

酪梨豆腐 | CHILLED TOFU AND AVOCADO

【 4人份 】

大酪梨...1個

豆腐...150公克(4兩)

醬油膏...2大匙

1 酪梨去皮、去籽後與豆腐分別切塊或兩者一起壓碎後置盤，酌量淋上醬油膏即可食用。

■ 酪梨選軟硬適中的既好處理也較好吃。喜食辣味者可在醬油膏內酌量加入芥末醬。

【 SERVES 4 】

1 large avocado

⅓ lb. (150g) tofu, regular

2 T. soy paste

1 Peel avocado and remove seed. Cut tofu and avocado into bite sized pieces or mash them together and place on a plate. Pour on soy paste and serve.

■ Avocado that is not too hard or too soft is easier to prepare and is best to use in this dish. Mustard may be added to soy paste for a spicy flavor.

茶葉蛋

【 12個 】

蛋...12個	
① 醬油...6大匙	
鹽...1 小匙	
糖...1大匙	
紅茶袋...3包(或其他茶葉)	
② 八角、桂皮、花椒、陳皮、 小茴、沙薑、丁香、豆蔻 ...各½大匙	

1 水滿過蛋，先煮滾再改中火煮4分鐘，熄火待微溫時即可敲裂蛋殼。

2 將煮好的蛋及①料、②料放入鍋內，加入6杯水至滿過蛋，燒開後改小火以微滾的火侯煮10分鐘，熄火靜置浸泡讓它入味，一天燒煮2次，隔天同法燒煮再浸泡，至蛋表面呈深咖啡色即可。

■ 浸泡蛋的時間需足夠才能讓滷汁的香味及鹹味滲透至蛋內。除上述方式外，敲裂殼的蛋亦可用慢鍋細火浸煮約8小時。

TEA EGGS

[12 EGGS]

12 eggs	
① 6 T. soy sauce	
1 t. salt	
1 T. sugar	
3 tea bags (black tea)	
② ½ T. ea.: star anise, cinnamon, Szechwan peppercorns, dried orange peels, cumin, galangal, cloves, nutmeg	

1 Use enough water to cover the eggs; bring to boil. Turn to medium heat and cook for 4 minutes then turn off. Let cool to room temperature. Lightly tap eggs so that shells will crack slightly.

2 Place eggs with ① and ② in a pot; add 6 c. water to cover eggs. Bring to boil, reduce heat to low and low boil for 10 minutes. Turn off heat; let eggs soak to absorb taste and to cool. Turn up heat and low boil again for 10 minutes. Turn heat off, let soak until cool. Repeat the boiling and cooling procedures twice a day until the shells turn dark brown.

■ The eggs need to be completely soaked in the salted and fragrant brew for a sufficient time for optimal flavor to permeate the eggs. The gently cracked eggs can also be simmered continuously in a crock pot for 8 hours low-heat, as an alternative to Step 2.

滷牛腱

【 6人份 】

牛腱...900公克(1½斤)

① 醬油...½杯
水...5杯
酒...¼杯
糖...2大匙
八角...½朵

1　牛腱先入滾水內川燙撈出，加①料燒開並改小火蓋鍋續煮約2小時至筷子能將肉插透即可撈出，煮時中途需翻面，待涼後切片淋上麻油、醬油膏或辣椒醬，隨意撒上蔥花、香菜。

■　利用①料可滷雞腿、雞鴨翅、內臟等，滷肉餘汁可滷豆干(10分鐘)、海帶(20分鐘)、蛋(30分鐘)，蛋可浸泡在滷汁內隔夜以便入味。滷味適於置冰箱分次食用。

BRAISED BEEF SHANK IN SOY SAUCE

【 SERVES 6 】

2 lb. (900g) beef shank

① ½ c. soy sauce
5 c. water
¼ c. cooking wine
2 T. sugar
½ star anise

1　Braise shank in boiling water; discard water. Add ① and bring to boil, turn heat to low and cook for 2 hours or until a chopstick can penetrate meat easily; remove. Turn meat several times during cooking. Slice meat when it cools down. Pour on sesame oil, soy sauce or chili sauce; sprinkle on cilantro and chopped green onions, as desired. Serve.

■　Mixture ① may be used to stew chicken legs, chicken wings, or giblets. Sauce from stewing meat can be used to cook pressed bean curd for 10 minutes, seaweed for 20 minutes, or eggs (boiled and shelled) for 30 minutes. Keeping the stewed eggs in the stewing sauce overnight will help the eggs absorb the flavor. All stewed ingredients may be refrigerated and used in portions several times.

叉燒肉

【 2人份 】

豬前腿肉...450公克(12兩)

1 | 蜂蜜、麥芽糖或糖...3大匙
酒、醬油、甜麵醬...各1½大匙
鹽...1小匙

1 將肉切4公分寬之長條,調入①料醃數小時或隔夜至入味。

2 烤箱燒熱,將醃好的肉條放入烤盤,置烤箱中層以200℃(400℉)烤約40分鐘,取出隨意刷上蜂蜜,待稍涼後切片食用。

■ 叉燒通常在廣式燒臘店有現成出售,色紅是添加食用色素之故。叉燒肉可隨喜好與蒜或香菜配食,也可沾醬油、辣椒醬或芥末醬等食用。叉燒肉除當小菜外也可趁熱以牛排吃法邊切邊食當主菜食用。

CANTONESE BBQ PORK

【 SERVES 2 】

1 lb. (450g) shoulder pork

1 | 3 T. honey, maltose or sugar
1½ T. ea.: cooking wine, soy sauce, sweet bean paste
1 t. salt

1 Cut meat into 1½"(4 cm) wide strips; add ① and marinate for several hours or overnight.

2 Preheat oven to 400°F(200°C); put meat on a roasting pan and cook on middle rack for 40 minutes. Remove. Brush on honey and let cool; cut to thin slices and serve as a side dish.

■ Cantonese BBQ Pork (Cha-Shiu) is readily available in Cantonese restaurants and delis. The red coloring is achieved with food coloring additives. Barbequed pork can be enjoyed with garlic or cilantro, or dipped in soy sauce, chili sauce, or mustard. In addition to serving the BBQ pork as a side dish as above. It can also be served as a one dish meal main dish by leaving strips whole and served while hot.

蚵仔煎

【 4人份 】

| 生蚵...450公克(12兩) |
| 茼蒿菜...450公克(12兩) |
| 雞蛋...4個 |

1
- 蕃薯粉...1¼杯，酒...1大匙
- 水...3杯，胡椒...½小匙
- 鹽...1小匙，韭菜(切1公分)...1杯

2
- 海鮮醬...½杯，番茄醬...¼杯
- 玉米粉、麻油...各1大匙
- 水...1杯，糖...¼杯

1　生蚵洗淨，瀝乾水份，若使用大蚵要先川燙再略切。1料調好，連同生蚵，茼蒿菜、雞蛋等各分4等份。將2料燒開當沾料。

2　油2大匙燒熱，將蚵散撒於鍋內煎1分鐘，將1份1料倒入鍋內，轉動鍋子使其成為大餅狀略煎待凝固時放入蛋液，再放茼蒿菜翻面煎熟後，趁熱淋上沾料。也可隨喜好加辣椒醬配食。同法做其餘3份。

■　可用小白菜、豆芽菜、西生菜或菠菜等取代茼蒿菜。蔥或香菜可取代韭菜。沾料可改用現成的甜辣醬或美式海鮮沾醬。

TAIWANESE OYSTER FRITTERS

【 SERVES 4 】

| 1 lb. (450g) oysters |
| 1 lb. (450g) tong ho |
| 4 eggs |

1
- 1¼ c. potato starch; 1 T. cooking wine; 3 c. water
- ½ t. pepper; 1 t. salt
- 1 c. Chinese chives, cut in ½" (1 cm) pieces

2
- ½ c. hoisin sauce
- 1 T. ea.: cornstarch, sesame oil
- ¼ c. ea.: ketchup, sugar
- 1 c. water

1　Wash oysters and drain. (If large oysters are used, briefly cook in boiling water then cut into smaller pieces.) Mix 1 and set aside. Divide oysters, 1, vegetables and eggs into four portions. Boil 2 for dipping sauce; set aside.

2　Heat 2 T. oil; spread one portion of oysters into wok; fry for 1 minute; pour a portion of 1 on top. Move wok in a circular motion to create a large "pancake"; cook until slightly firm. Add one lightly beaten egg then a vegetable portion; turn over and fry until cooked, remove immediately. Serve with dipping sauce while it is hot. Add chili sauce as desired. Repeat the same procedures to make the remaining three fritters.

■　Short bok choy, bean sprouts, lettuce, or spinach may be used for tong ho. Green onions or cilantro may be substituted for Chinese chives. Cocktail sauce may be used instead of 2 to simplify the procedures.

鹽酥雞

【 4人份 】

雞胸或雞腿肉...300公克(8兩)
① 酒、蒜末...各1大匙
鹽、五香粉...各⅛匙
糖...1小匙
醬油...1大匙
蕃薯粉或玉米粉...½杯
炸油...4杯
九層塔...隨意
② 椒鹽...½小匙
辣椒粉...隨意

1　雞肉切2 x 3公分塊，調入①料醃20分鐘後，沾上蕃薯粉備炸。

2　油燒熱，入雞塊以中火炸4~5分鐘至金黃色，加入九層塔略炸後立即撈出，拌入②料即可。

■　魷魚、生蚵等海鮮可取代雞肉，做成鹽酥魷魚或鹽酥蚵。在專業賣鹽酥雞的攤上通常還附帶賣炸甜不辣、魚丸、花枝丸、雞內臟或蔬菜等，這是台灣最受歡迎的小吃之一。

CRISPY CHICKEN WITH PEPPER SALT

[SERVES 4]

⅔ lb. (300g) chicken breast or boneless chicken legs
① 1 T. ea.: cooking wine, minced garlic
⅛ t. ea.: salt, five spices powder
1 t. sugar; 1 T. soy sauce
½ c. potato starch or cornstarch
4 c. oil for deep-frying
basil as desired
② ½ t. pepper salt
chili powder as desired

1　Wash chicken and cut into ¾" x 1¼" (2 cm x 3 cm) pieces; marinate in ① for 20 minutes. Coat with potato starch and set aside.

2　Heat oil for deep-frying; fry chicken over medium heat for 4 or 5 minutes, until golden in color. Add cilantro and briefly fry; remove chicken and basil immediately. Mix with ②. Serve.

■　Seafood, such as squid and oysters, may be cooked the same way to make the famous Taiwanese style crispy squid and crispy oysters. The street vendors who specialize in crispy chicken usually sell a variety of fried fish cakes, fish balls, cuttlefish balls, vegetables, etc. This dish is one of the most popular Taiwanese street vendor foods.

紅油抄手　SZECHWAN WON TONS

【 四川菜 】　　　　　　【 2人份 】

餛飩...20個

1 醬油...6大匙
　糖、醋...各1大匙
　蒜泥...2大匙

2 蔥末、辣油...各2大匙

1　將 1 料調勻備用。

2　多量水燒開，放入餛飩後略為攪動以防黏鍋，待餛飩全部浮起見肉熟撈出盛盤，酌量將 1 料淋在餛飩上，再加 2 料即成。

餛飩湯 罐頭雞湯2杯加水3杯煮滾，放入20個餛飩煮熟後熄火，加醬油、麻油、胡椒、海苔、蔥花等。

【 SZECHWAN CUISINE 】　　　　　　【 SERVES 2 】

20 won tons

1 **6 T. soy sauce**
　1 T. ea.: sugar, vinegar
　2 T. ground garlic

2 **2 T. ea.: minced green onion, chili oil**

1　Mix 1 and set aside.

2　Boil enough water to cook won tons. Put won tons in boiling water and lightly stir to prevent them from sticking to the pot. Cook until won tons rise to the surface and meat is cooked; remove. Add the desired portions of 1 and 2 to the won tons and serve.

WON TON SOUP Bring 2 c. canned chicken broth and 3 c. water to boil. Add 20 won tons and boil until cooked. Turn off heat; add soy sauce, sesame oil, pepper, seaweed, and chopped green onions as desired. Serve.

餛飩作法　HOW TO MAKE WON TONS

【 80個 】

薄餛飩皮...80片(450公克，12兩)

1 絞肉*...450公克(12兩)
　鹽、醬油、糖...各1½小匙
　胡椒...¼小匙
　酒、麻油...各1大匙
　蛋(打散)... 2個

1　將 1 料略拌，蛋分數次加入，用力順同一方向攪拌均勻成餡。

2　將餡放在餛飩皮中間，折成三角型(圖1)壓扁，煮時較易熟，再折一次(圖2)，兩端沾水捏緊(圖3)放在鋪有紙巾的盤上，並依序將全部餛飩做好備用。

*　絞肉宜買前腿肉現絞(略帶肥肉才好吃)，若使用較瘦的絞肉則需多加麻油。

【 MAKES 80 】

80 won ton skins (thin), 1 lb. (450g)

1 **1 lb (450g) ground pork***
　1½ t. ea.: salt, soy sauce, sugar
　¼ t. pepper
　1 T. ea.: cooking wine, sesame oil
　2 eggs, beaten

1　Mix 1; add eggs gradually and continue to mix well, stirring in the same direction to make the filling for 80 won tons.

2　Put a portion of filling in the center of a won ton skin and fold corner over to make a triangle (Fig. 1); lightly flatten so the filling will cook evenly. Fold over again (Fig. 2). Moisten the ends with water and press together (Fig. 3) and place on a paper towel. Follow the same procedure to make the remaining 79 won tons.

*　Won tons taste best when using ground meat with some fat. If lean meat is used, increase the amount of sesame oil in 1.

炸豆腐 | CRISPY TOFU WITH GARLIC SAUCE

【 4人份 】

嫩豆腐...450公克(12兩)

① 醬油膏...3大匙，蒜泥...1大匙

炸油...4杯

1 豆腐切塊並擦乾水份，①料拌勻備用。

2 油燒熱，入豆腐以大火炸約4分鐘至金黃酥脆時撈出，瀝乾油後盛盤，酌量淋上①料後趁熱食用。

■ 炸豆腐也可沾椒鹽食用。

【 SERVES 4 】

1 lb (450g) tofu, soft

① **3 T. soy paste**

1 T. ground garlic

4 c. oil for deep-frying

1 Cut tofu into pieces, pat dry with a paper towel. Mix ① and set aside.

2 Heat oil and deep-fry tofu 4 minutes over high heat until crispy and golden. Remove and drain. Place on a plate, pour on ①; serve while hot.

■ This dish tastes best when served with pepper salt.

烤花生 | ROASTED PEANUTS

帶皮生花生...½杯，鹽...隨意

1 將花生略沖水瀝乾，表面略潮濕時撒入少許鹽，不加蓋用微波爐加熱1½分鐘，略翻拌一下再加熱40秒至微黃。若試吃尚有生味可再放入加熱，待完全冷卻後即香脆可口。

■ 以微波爐烤花生，不要一次加熱過久，以免太焦會有苦味。

½ c. peanuts, shelled

salt as desired

1 Rinse peanuts and while the skin is moist, sprinkle on some salt. Microwave uncovered for 1½ minutes. Remove and stir lightly. Put back in microwave for another 40 seconds until slightly brown. If peanuts still taste raw, microwave again until done. Remove and let cool so peanuts can become crunchy. Serve.

■ Do not overheat in microwave; separately heat the peanuts in two or three repetitions to avoid burning the peanuts, making them bitter.

丸子湯

絞豬腿肉...300公克(8兩)

1.
鹽...½小匙
糖、胡椒、麻油...各¼匙
蛋白...1個
酒、玉米粉...各1大匙

2.
罐頭雞湯...2杯
水...3杯

3.
胡椒、麻油...隨意
芹菜末(或香菜)...4大匙

1 絞肉調入1料順同一方向攪拌至有黏性。

2 將2料燒開後改小火，以手抓起絞肉，並握拳擠出丸子，以湯匙沾水以防粘匙，挖出後立即投入2料中，待丸子全部放入後，改大火煮至丸子浮出水面去除泡沫，加入3料即成。

■ 可任意用牛肉、魚肉、花枝肉或蝦仁取代豬絞肉做出各式丸子，用來煮湯、清蒸、油炸或紅燒均適宜。

TAIWANESE MEAT BALL SOUP

[SERVES 4]

⅔ lb (300g) ground pork

1.
½ t. salt; 1 egg white
¼ t. ea.: sugar, pepper, sesame oil
1 T. ea.: cornstarch, cooking wine

2. 2 c. canned chicken broth; 3 c. water

3.
pepper and sesame oil as desired
4 T. minced celery or cilantro

1 Add 1 to the meat and stir in one direction until sticky to make a meat paste.

2 Boil 2 then reduce heat to low. To form a meatball, take some meat in your hand and squeeze the mixture firmly to force up a meat ball between the thumb and forefinger. Using a wet spoon (to avoid sticking), scoop the meat ball from the hand and put in 2 one by one until all meat balls are in the broth. Turn heat to high and cook until meat balls rise to the surface. Skim off surface foam with a spoon; add 3, and serve.

■ Ground beef, fish fillet, cuttlefish or shrimp may be substituted for pork to make meat balls or seafood balls. There are many ways to cook the balls, they can be steamed, deep-fried, cooked in soy sauce, or used in soup.

酸辣湯

【 4人份 】

肉絲(豬、牛或雞)...½杯

1┌ 酒、醬油、玉米粉...各1小匙

豆腐...150公克(4兩)

2┌ 罐頭雞湯...2杯，水...3杯

3┌ 香菇絲、木耳絲、筍絲或金針*
　└ ...共¾杯

4┌ 玉米粉...3大匙，水...4大匙

蛋(打散)...2個

5┌ 醬油、醋...各2大匙
　│ 胡椒...⅛小匙，麻油...1小匙
　└ 蔥絲、薑絲、香菜末...各1大匙

1　肉絲先調上①料略醃，豆腐切絲備用。

2　將②料燒開，放入肉絲並攪散，續入豆腐絲及③料再燒開，以調勻的④料勾芡成濃汁，待滾後徐徐淋入蛋液略攪動使其散開，立即熄火並加上⑤料即成。

*　香菇、木耳、金針應先泡軟去蒂再使用。

■　肉絲可用現成的叉燒肉絲(見145頁)或其他熟肉絲取代不需再用①料醃拌。若無③料可將豆腐份量增加至225公克(6兩)，做成簡易酸辣湯。

HOT AND SOUR SOUP

【 SERVES 4 】

½ c. shredded pork, beef or chicken

1┌ 1 t. ea.: cooking wine, soy sauce, cornstarch

⅓ lb (150g) tofu

2┌ 2 c. canned chicken broth; 3 c. water

3┌ ¾ c. (total): lily buds, shredded Chinese black mushrooms,
　└ 　wood ears or bamboo shoots*

4┌ 3 T. cornstarch; 4 T. water

2 eggs, slightly beaten

5┌ 2 T. ea.: soy sauce, vinegar
　│ ⅓ t. pepper; 1 t. sesame oil
　└ 1 T. ea.: minced cilantro, shredded green onion and ginger root

1　Marinate meat in ①. Cut tofu into strips and set aside.

2　Boil ②, add meat and stir to separate; add tofu and ③. Bring to a boil and add mixture ④ to thicken. When boiling, slowly add eggs in a thin stream, stir lightly and let eggs spread. Immediately turn heat off; add ⑤ and serve.

*　Soak lily buds, Chinese black mushrooms and wood ears in cold water until soft, remove stems then shred.

■　If ready-made Cantonese BBQ pork (p.145) or cooked meat shreds are used, there is no need to marinate the meat in ①. To simplify the procedures of this dish, omit ③ and increase the amount of tofu to ½ lb. (225g).

玉米羹

【 4人份 】

罐頭玉米醬...2杯

☐1 罐頭雞湯...2杯
水...2杯

☐2 豬或雞絞肉、洋菇、蘆筍、
玉米粒...任選½杯

☐3 玉米粉...3大匙
水...3大匙

蛋(打散)...2個
麻油...½小匙

1 將玉米醬及☐1料燒開，加入☐2
料攪拌燒開，隨即加入拌勻的
☐3料攪拌燒開呈糊狀，最後徐
徐淋入蛋液略攪動使其散開，
加麻油即成。可隨意撒上蔥
花、胡椒等。

玉米濃湯 先將奶油、洋蔥末及
麵粉各5大匙炒成麵糊，加入
玉米醬罐頭攪拌後再入☐1料攪
勻燒開即成。因為湯內有炒過
的麵粉，味道更為香濃，不需
再加☐3料勾芡。蛋液及☐2料可
隨喜好加入。

CHINESE CORN SOUP

[SERVES 4]

2 c. canned cream style sweet corn

☐1 2 c. canned chicken broth
2 c. water

☐2 ½ c. total (optional): ground pork or chicken, mushrooms,
asparagus, corn kernels

☐3 3 T. cornstarch
3 T. water

2 eggs, slightly beaten
½ t. sesame oil

1 Bring canned corn and ☐1 to boil; add ☐2 and bring to boil again.
Add mixture ☐3, stir until thickened. Slowly add eggs in a small
stream, stir continuously to let eggs spread. Add sesame oil and
serve. Chopped green onions and pepper may be added as
desired. Serve.

CREAMY CORN CHOWDER Stir-fry
5 T. each of butter, minced
onion and flour to make a paste.
Add sweet corn and stir to mix;
add ☐1 and mix well. Bring to
boil then serve. Stir-frying flour
with butter makes an aromatic
and flavory creamy soup. There
is no need to add ☐3 to thicken.
Beaten eggs and ☐2 may be
added as desired.

米 小菜
CHINESE RICE 麵
NOODLES APPETIZERS
簡 SOUPS
餐 SWEETS 湯
甜點

銀耳蓮子湯

【 4人份 】

白木耳(銀耳)...1大朵(或⅔杯)

蓮子(乾)...½杯

糖...6大匙

1 將白木耳浸泡於水中，脹大展開後(圖1)撈出去蒂切小朵。

2 白木耳與蓮子加水5杯煮開，以小火蓋鍋煮約30分鐘或煮至鬆軟，最後加糖煮開即可。

■ 市售白木耳品質不同，煮時若覺白木耳太爛可先撈出，等蓮子鬆軟後再將木耳放回湯內。蓮子的品質也會影響煮的時間長短，可視個人喜好口感調整。

■ 白木耳潤肺養氣，蓮子健脾養胃，可單煮一種，也可隨喜好加入紅棗、枸杞、百合等，冷熱食皆可。

SWEET LOTUS SEEDS AND SILVER WOOD EAR

【 SERVES 4 】

1 white wood ear, approx. ⅔ c.

½ c. lotus seeds

6 T. sugar

1 Soak wood ear in cold water until expanded (Fig. 1). Remove; cut off hard ends and cut into pieces.

2 Combine wood ears, lotus seeds and 5 c. water; bring to a boil. Turn heat to low, cover and simmer for 30 minutes or until lotus seeds soften. Add sugar, bring to boil again; turn off heat and serve.

■ The quality of white wood ears sold in stores may vary. Some soften quickly when boiled; if so, remove wood ears during cooking and return when lotus seeds are softened. Also, the grade of lotus seeds can affect the optimal cooking time. Cooking time may be adjusted according to individual preference.

■ White wood ears are thought to lubricate the lungs and nourish one's Chi or "life force." Lotus seeds can increase one's appetite and strengthen the stomach. The dessert may contain just one item or be enhanced with additional ingredients such as red jujubes, lycium berries, or lily buds. This dessert may be served hot or cold.

芋頭椰奶西米露

西谷米(圖1)...½杯	
① 芋頭(切丁)...1½杯	
水...4杯	
糖...½杯	
椰漿...½杯	

1　將①料燒開，改中火煮約10分鐘待芋頭熟透，再加糖½杯煮至糖溶化，倒入椰漿即刻熄火。

2　水3杯煮開，入西谷米煮滾後，改中火續煮約4分鐘見中間白色外層呈透明狀，即可撈出，倒入煮好的芋頭甜湯內，西谷米會吸水而透明，冷熱食均可。

■　芋頭可改用蕃薯或去殼綠豆等，也可數種材料混合使用。若無椰漿可用奶水。

TARO TAPIOCA WITH COCONUT MILK

【 SERVES 4 】

½ c. tapioca balls (Fig. 1)	
① 1½ c. taro root, diced	
4 c. water	
½ c. sugar	
½ c. coconut milk	

1　Boil ①, reduce heat to medium and simmer 10 minutes until taro is cooked. Add sugar and continue to cook until sugar is melted. Pour in coconut milk; turn heat off immediately.

2　Boil 3 c. water, add tapioca and bring to a boil again. Reduce heat to medium and simmer for 4 minutes until tapioca exterior becomes translucent and center remains white. Immediately place the tapioca in taro liquid so it absorbs water and becomes transparent. May be served either hot or cold.

■　Yams, sweet potatoes, or skinless mung beans may be used instead of taro root and may be used alone or mixed. Evaporated milk may be used instead of coconut milk.

桂圓紫米粥

【 4人份 】

黑糯米...¼杯

白糯米...¼杯

桂圓肉(龍眼乾，圖1)...3大匙

糖...¼杯

1　黑糯米用水浸泡隔夜後瀝乾，加水4杯煮開，改中火煮12分鐘，放入白糯米及桂圓肉燒開再煮12分鐘，續入糖攪拌至溶化即可。

■　粥不要煮太稠，熄火靜置數分鐘後，米會吸收水份而更加濃稠。黑糯米較不具黏性，故宜與白糯米一起煮。

八寶粥　白糯米內隨意加入多種材料如紅豆、綠豆、花生、蓮子、桂圓肉、紅棗、薏仁等煮熟即成八寶粥，煮時不易熟的材料可先煮，易熟的材料後加，全部煮熟後再入適量的糖即可。

SWEET PURPLE RICE WITH LONGAN

[SERVES 4]

¼ c. black glutinous rice (purple rice)

¼ c. white glutinous rice

3 T. longan, pitted (Fig. 1)

¼ c. sugar

1　Soak black glutinous rice in water overnight; drain. Add 4 c. water and bring to a boil; turn heat to medium and cook for 12 minutes. Add white glutinous rice and longan; bring to a boil and cook for 12 minutes. Add sugar and stir until sugar has melted. Serve.

■　Do not overcook congee because it will absorb water and thicken in a few minutes after turning off heat. Purple rice is not as sticky as glutinous rice; it is best to mix and cook them together.

EIGHT-TREASURED SWEET CONGEE

The name "eight-treasure" comes from cooking many different kinds of ingredients with glutinous rice. Red beans, mung beans, peanuts, lotus seeds, pitted longan, red dates, barley, etc. are good choices for making this popular sweet congee. Cook the ingredients that need the most cooking time first, then add other ingredients according to their necessary cooking time; finally add sugar as desired.

芝麻糊

炒熟黑芝麻...1¼杯

1 {
水...3杯
糖...¼杯
}

2 {
玉米粉...1½大匙
水...1½大匙
}

1　黑芝麻加1杯水放入果汁機內攪碎成糊狀，再加 1 料燒滾，立即以拌勻的 2 料勾芡至喜歡的濃稠度即可。

■　堅果類在使用前若先炒熟或烤熟則味道較香。

花生糊　將熟花生(見150頁)去皮後取代黑芝麻，其他材料與作法同上。也可改用腰果、核桃或栗子代替花生。

CREAMY ROASTED BLACK SESAME

〔 SERVES 4 〕

1¼ c. black sesame seeds, roasted

1 {
3 c. water
¼ c. sugar
}

2 {
1½ T. cornstarch
1½ T. water
}

1　Add 1 c. water to sesame seeds and put in a blender; grind to a fine and creamy consistency. In a saucepan, put 1 and bring to boil; add mixture 2 and stir to thicken as desired. Serve.

■　Toasting or roasting nuts before using them in this recipe will enhance the fragrance of this dish.

CREAMY ROASTED PEANUTS
Replace sesame seeds with roasted skinless peanuts (p. 150). Other ingredients and procedure is the same. Cashews or walnuts may also be used for this recipe.

紅豆湯

紅豆... 2杯

糖...⅔杯

1 紅豆加水10杯煮開後改小火蓋鍋煮約1小時或至紅豆裂開即可加糖，若湯汁太稀可調玉米粉水勾芡成薄汁。

■ 紅豆為紅豆樹的種籽，含多量食物纖維與維生素，市面上以袋裝出售。紅豆除可煮紅豆湯之外，亦可壓成泥製成紅豆沙，為中式甜點的主要材料。

紅豆圓仔湯 將湯圓放入滾水內煮到浮起撈出，放入紅豆湯內即成。

蕃薯紅豆湯 紅豆湯熄火前5分鐘將蕃薯塊放入，再加糖。

紅豆牛奶冰 煮紅豆時水份減少，煮到汁略收乾，待冰涼後加上刨冰及煉乳。

RED BEAN DESSERT

2 c. red beans

⅔ c. sugar

1 Bring 10 c. water and the red beans to a boil; turn heat to low, cover and cook for 1 hour or until beans crack open. Add sugar; add cornstarch if liquid is too thin.

■ Rich in vitamins and fiber, red beans are the seeds of red bean trees. Sold in packages at Chinese markets, red beans can also be boiled and mashed into bean paste which forms the main filling for many delectable Chinese pastries.

RED BEAN AND RICE BALL DESSERT
Place sticky rice balls into boiling water until they float; remove them with slotted spoon and place into cooked red bean dessert soup. Frozen sticky rice balls are sold in the frozen section of Chinese supermarkets.

RED BEAN AND YAM DESSERT
Add pieces of yam 5 minutes prior to doneness of the red beans; add sugar.

RED BEANS TOPPED WITH SHAVED ICE AND MILK Reduce the water used to boil red beans and cook until liquid is almost evaporated. After cooling, top with shaved ice and milk.

花生湯

PEANUT DESSERT

【 8人份 】

去皮生花生...2杯

糖...⅔杯

1 花生及水8杯放入快鍋內煮開後轉小火煮1小時，熄火燜約20分鐘後開蓋，加入糖再燒開即成。冷、熱食皆宜。

■ 花生軟綿才好吃，一般的花生不易煮軟，宜用快鍋來煮。

花生豆花 食用時將花生湯加在豆花上即成，是台灣有名的小吃(市面上有現成的豆花出售)。

【 SERVES 8 】

2 c. blanched peanuts

⅔ c. sugar

1 Add peanuts to 8 c. water in a pressure cooker; bring to boil and turn heat to low. Cook 1 hour. Turn off heat. Let set 20 minutes then open pressure cooker and add sugar; bring to a boil again. May serve hot or cold.

■ This recipe requires peanuts to be cooked until very soft to produce the best taste. Since peanuts take a long time to cook, it is best to use a pressure cooker.

DO-HWA WITH PEANUT DESSERT
Put the Peanut Dessert on the soybean "flower" (Do-Hwa) and serve. This is one of the most popular Taiwanese street vendor foods. Ready-made soybean flower (Do-Hwa) is available in Asian supermarkets.

綠豆湯　MUNG BEAN DESSERT

【 4人份 】

【 SERVES 4 】

1　綠豆...1杯

糖...6大匙

1 c. mung beans

6 T. sugar

1　將綠豆與水6杯燒開，以中火煮20分鐘或至喜好的軟度*，再加糖煮至糖溶化即熄火，冷熱食皆宜。

*　傳說若將綠豆煮熟但皮未裂開之前即熄火，煮出來的綠豆湯有消暑退火功效，適合炎夏食用。若希望綠豆更軟，可延長煮的時間。

1　Bring mung beans and 6 cups of water to boil; turn to medium heat and cook for 20 minutes or more for desired softness*. Stir in sugar; turn off heat when sugar is dissolved. Serve hot or cold.

*　To get full body cooling benefits, do not let bean pods open up by cooking too long. This soup is best served in summer. If very soft beans are preferred, increase cooking time to allow the bean pods to open.

綠豆涼糕　MUNG BEAN "CUBIES"

【 4人份 】

【 SERVES 4 】

1　熟綠豆仁*(圖1)...2杯

水...½杯

吉利丁...1½大匙(14公克)

2 c. cooked skinless mung beans* (Fig. 1)

½ c. water

1½ T. (½ oz, 14g) unflavored gelatin

1　將1料放入果汁機打成綠豆泥。

2　吉利丁加入1杯水中置1分鐘再以小火慢慢加熱，攪拌至吉利丁完全溶解後熄火，續入綠豆泥攪拌均勻，倒入容器內待涼，置冰箱凝固。

*　綠豆仁的煮法：綠豆仁(去皮的綠豆)1杯與水5杯燒開，改中火煮15分鐘，至湯汁略收乾，加糖⅔杯煮至溶化即成，熄火待涼後，水份會吸收到豆內，約可得3杯。

綠豆牛奶冰沙 熟綠豆仁1杯與鮮奶1 1/4杯及冰塊5塊一起放入果汁機打勻。煮熟的紅豆、芋頭或花生可取代熟綠豆仁做成不同口味的冰沙。

1　Liquefy 1 in a blender.

2　Stir gelatin into 1 c. water and let stand for 1 minute. Heat over low heat and stir until gelatin is dissolved; turn off heat. Stir mung bean liquid into the gelatin and mix well; pour into another container to cool. Place in refrigerator until firm to the touch. Serve cold.

*　To cook skinless mung beans: Place 5 cups of water and 1 cup skinless mung beans in a pot, bring to a boil and turn to medium heat; cook for 15 minutes until liquid is almost evaporated. Stir in ⅔ cup of sugar; turn off heat and let cool to absorb liquid. This will result in three cups of cooked mung beans.

MUNG BEAN MILK SLUSH Liquefy 1 cup of cooked skinless mung beans, 1¼ cup of milk and 5 ice cubes in a blender. Mung beans may be substituted with cooked red beans, taro root or peanuts for a different taste.

芋頭涼糕

【 4人份 】

去皮芋頭*... 225公克(6兩)	
①{ 牛奶...1杯	
椰奶...½杯	
吉利丁...1½大匙(14g)	
煮芋頭的湯汁...⅔杯	
糖... ½杯	

1　芋頭切1公分薄片加2杯水煮開，改小火煮到熟軟撈出與①料用果汁機攪勻成芋奶。鍋內保留⅔杯煮芋頭的湯汁待涼備用。

2　將吉利丁加入煮芋頭的湯汁內靜置1分鐘，隨入糖以小火加熱並攪拌至吉利丁溶化，再加入芋奶攪拌均勻繼續加熱數分鐘至微溫即熄火，倒入容器中待涼，放冰箱冷藏數小時至凝結即可。

＊　若購買帶皮芋頭(圖1)，需先去皮再使用。

■　牛奶不適合高溫烹煮，故加熱時用小火加熱攪拌均勻即可，不必燒滾。

TARO JELLO

【 SERVES 4 】

½ lb. (225g) pared taro root*	
①{ 1 c. milk; ½ c. coconut milk	
1½ T. (½ oz., 14g) unflavored gelatin	
⅔ c. liquid reserved from cooking taro	
½ c. sugar	

1　Slice taro in ⅜" (1 cm) thickness then place in a pot with 2 c. water; bring to a boil and turn heat to low, cook until taro is soft. Drain and reserve ⅔ c. of liquid; set aside and let cool to room temperature. Place sliced taro in a blender together with ①; liquefy to make taro milk.

2　Stir gelatin into reserved liquid and let stand 1 minute. Place mixture over low heat and stir in sugar until gelatin dissolves. Pour in taro milk and continue stirring over low heat until warm to the touch; turn off heat. Pour into serving container, let cool to room temperature. Transfer to refrigerator and let stand until firm.

＊　If taro root with skin (Fig.1) is purchased, pare the taro before use.

■　Use low heat to cook taro milk and check constantly to prevent boiling the milk.

焦糖雞蛋布丁

[8個]

① 糖...½杯
水...1大匙

蛋...3個

② 香草精...½小匙
鮮奶...2杯，糖...¼杯

1　以中火將①料燒至糖溶化，改小火略炒至褐色成焦糖，趁熱倒入8個小烤模內，使均勻佈滿底部(圖1)，待涼備用。

2　蛋打勻與②料混合攪拌均勻，倒入有焦糖的烤模內，置於烤盤上，加熱水至烤模之半腰處，烤箱燒熱以160℃(325°F)烤約15分鐘，至表面鼓起，取出烤模冰涼約3小時。

3　食時以刀子在布丁邊緣劃一圈，上置盤再倒扣於盤上即可。

■　模型的材質、大小、厚薄會影響烘烤時間，讀者可自行調整。

巧克力布丁　將②料改為2杯巧克力牛奶，其餘材料及作法同上。

FLAN WITH CARAMEL

[MAKES 8 SERVINGS]

① ½ c. sugar; 1 T. water

3 eggs

② ½ t. vanilla extract
2 c. milk
¼ c. sugar

1　Heat ① over medium heat until sugar is melted, stir if necessary. Reduce heat to low and cook until syrup turns a light golden brown color. Immediately pour into 8 molds (Fig. 1). Let cool.

2　Beat eggs and add ②, blend well and pour into the 8 molds. Set flan molds in a baking pan, add hot water to halfway up the sides of flan mold. Bake uncovered in an oven at 325°F(160°C) for 15 minutes, or until top rises a little bit. Remove and let cool. Refrigerate for 3 hours.

3　To serve, run a knife around the edges to free the flan. Place a serving dish on top of molds, hold together and turn over to let flan drop on the dish.

■　The size, thickness, and quality of the molds for flan may affect the baking time. Readers should adjust baking time accordingly.

CHOCOLATE FLAN Substitute ingredients ② with 2 cups of chocolate milk, other ingredients and procedures remain the same.

【 4個 】

紅茶袋或綠茶袋...4個

① 吉利丁...1½大匙(14g)
水...½杯

糖... 6大匙

鮮奶油...適量

1 水2½杯燒熱，放入茶袋靜置數分鐘後取出。

2 將①料略拌後放置1分鐘，用小火加熱並攪拌至吉利丁完全溶解，續入糖攪拌溶解後熄火，再倒入熱茶攪勻，待涼後分置容器中，待涼後分置容器中，冷藏隔夜或至凝結。食時淋上鮮奶油更具風味！

咖啡凍 將1½大匙吉利丁拌入2¾杯水中置一分鐘，用中火將吉利丁煮溶，續入6大匙糖及4大匙即溶咖啡煮至糖溶化後熄火，待涼後分置容器中，冷藏至凝固，食前淋上鮮奶油。

ICED TEA JELLO

【 MAKES 4 】

4 tea bags: black tea, green tea, or herbal tea

① **1½ T. (½ oz., 14g) unflavored gelatin**
½ c. water

6 T. sugar

whipping cream as desire

1 Pour 2½ c. boiling water over tea bags; steep for 2 to 4 minutes. Remove tea bags.

2 Mix ① and let stand 1 minute. Stir over low heat until gelatin is dissolved. Pour in sugar and continue to stir until dissolved. Turn off heat and pour in hot tea; mix well. Let cool to room temperature, place in serving containers and place in refrigerator overnight until firm. Serve with whipping cream to enhance the flavor.

ICED COFFEE JELLO Stir 1½ T. of gelatin into 2¾ c. water, let stand 1 minute. Stir over medium heat until gelatin is dissolved. Add 6 T. sugar and 4 T. instant coffee, continue stirring until sugar is dissolved. Turn off heat and let cool. Place in serving containers and place in refrigerator until firm to the touch. Serve with whipping cream.

杏仁豆腐

【 4人份 】

1. 吉利丁...2大匙(18g)
   糖...⅓杯，水...1杯
2. 鮮奶...1½杯，杏仁精...1小匙
3. 糖...½杯，水...3杯
   水果罐頭...1罐(240公克)

1　將1料置鍋內以小火慢慢加熱，攪拌至完全溶解燒開即熄火，隨入2料攪拌均勻，倒入容器內待涼，置冰箱冷藏至凝結後即為杏仁豆腐。3料煮成糖水冰涼備用。

2　杏仁豆腐切小塊，隨喜好加入冰涼的糖水與什錦水果一起食用。

■　不同廠牌的吉利丁做出來的成品軟硬度不太相同，讀者可依個人喜好增減份量。

ALMOND JELLO

[SERVES 4]

1. 2 T. (18g) unflavored gelatin
   ⅓ c. sugar
   1 c. water
2. 1½ c. milk
   1 t. almond extract (more if desired)
3. ½ c. sugar
   3 c. water
   1 can mixed fruit, 8½ oz (240g)

■ Different gelatin brands produce different jello firmnesses and textures. Adjust amount of gelatin to suit personal taste.

1　Cook 1 in a pot over low heat and stir until mixture is dissolved; turn off heat. Stir in 2 and mix well; transfer to a serving container. Place in refrigerator and let stand until firm. Boil 3 and stir until sugar dissolves to make sugar water. Let cool, then refrigerate.

2　Slice Almond Jello into small cubes and serve with iced sugar water and mixed fruit.

香蕉牛奶

【 2人份 】

① 香蕉(去皮，切塊)...1支
牛奶...1¼杯，冰塊...隨意
蜂蜜或糖...2大匙

1 將香蕉與①料一起放入果汁機，先用慢速打碎冰塊，再轉高速將材料打勻即可。

哈密瓜牛奶 將1½杯的哈密瓜(切塊)與①料放入果汁機打勻。

木瓜牛奶 將1½杯的木瓜(切塊)與①料放入果汁機打勻。

藍莓蘋果奶昔

【 2人份 】

① 藍莓...½杯 (約70公克.)
蘋果(去皮切丁)...1個 (約1⅓杯)
香草冰淇淋...2球
牛奶...1杯
冰塊...隨意

1 將①料一起放入果汁機，先用慢速打碎冰塊，再轉高速將材料打勻即可。

BLUEBERRY APPLE MILK SHAKE

【 SERVES 2 】

① ½ c. (2½ oz, 70g) blueberry
1 apple (1⅛ c.), pared and diced
2 large scoops of vanilla ice cream
1 c. milk
ice cubes as desired

1 Place ① in a blender. Start with low speed to break up ice cubes, then turn to high speed and blend mixture until smooth.

BANANA MILK SMOOTHIE

【 SERVES 2 】

① 1 banana, peeled and cut into pieces
1¼ c. milk
ice cubes as desired
2 T. honey or sugar

1 Place ① and the banana in a blender; use low speed initially to break up the ice cubes. Increase speed to high to mix well.

CANTALOUPE MILK SMOOTHIE Cut cantaloupe into pieces to total 1½ c. Place in a blender with ①. Follow same procedures as above.

PAPAYA MILK SMOOTHIE Cut papaya into pieces to total 1½ c. Place in a blender with ①. Follow same procedures as above. This is a popular drink in Taiwan, and is sold in many independent and franchised cold drink stores.

香瓜凍飲

【 2人份 】

1
- 香瓜(切塊)...2杯(約300公克)
- 檸檬汁...1大匙
- 蜂蜜或糖...4大匙
- 水...½杯，冰塊...10塊

1 將1料一起放入果汁機，先用低速打碎冰塊，再轉高速將材料打勻即可得約3杯。

奇異果凍飲 將奇異果4個代替香瓜，其他材料與作法不變。

水果凍飲

【 2人份 】

1
- 香蕉(切塊)...1條
- 草莓... 3個(約½杯)
- 蘋果(去皮切塊)...½個(約½杯)
- 原味優格...1杯，檸檬汁...1小匙
- 水...½杯，糖...2大匙
- 冰塊...10塊

1 將1料一起放入果汁機，先用低速打碎冰塊，再轉高速將材料打勻即可得約3杯。

HONEYDEW SMOOTHIE

[SERVES 2]

1
- 2 c. (300g) Honeydew melon, diced
- 1 T. lemon juice
- 4 T. honey or sugar
- ½ c. water
- 10 ice cubes

1 Place 1 in a blender. Start with low speed to break up ice cubes. Increase speed to high to get smooth mixture to total 3 c.

KIWI SLUSH Use four kiwis instead of the honeydew. Follow the same procedures as above.

FRUIT SMOOTHIE

[SERVES 2]

1
- 1 Banana, peeled and cut into pieces
- 3 strawberries, approx. ½ c.
- ½ apple (½ c.), pared and diced
- 1 c. plain yogurt
- 1 t. lemon juice
- ½ c. water
- 2 T. sugar
- 10 ice cubes

1 Place 1 in a blender. Start with low speed to break up ice cubes. Increase speed to high to get smooth mixture to total 3 c.

珍珠奶茶 ｜ BOBA MILK TEA

粉圓*(圖1)...1杯

紅茶包...2包

1 ｜ 奶精...3大匙

蜂蜜或糖...⅓杯

冰塊...隨意

1 多量水燒開，依包裝指示將粉圓煮熟，撈起沖冷水，瀝乾備用。

2 水3杯燒熱，放入茶袋靜置數分鐘後取出，加入 1 料調勻成奶茶，待涼加入冰塊調成冰奶茶，再加入珍珠即成。珍珠奶茶冷熱飲皆宜。

* 粉圓因品牌而異，快煮粉圓可在10分鐘內煮好，乾粉圓則需要反覆煮爛數次，烹煮前需參考包裝說明。

■ 傳統珍珠奶茶的作法是將紅茶水、奶精、糖水、冰塊放入搖搖杯內，上下搖晃數十下成泡沫紅茶，再倒入裝有粉圓的杯中飲用。冰過的粉圓會變硬，所以煮好後最好當天食用。此種將奶茶與QQ的粉圓結合的飲料文化起源於臺灣，現已風行至各國，因粉圓像珍珠，於是取名為珍珠奶茶。後來流行使用更大顆的粉圓，故稱為波霸奶茶。

■ 珍珠奶茶的口味變化很多，可隨意添加紅豆、綠豆、椰果、咖啡凍丁。粉圓則可加入冰咖啡、泰式奶茶、港式凍鴛鴦（咖啡與奶茶各半）及花式水果冰沙飲料等。

水晶奶茶 將咖啡凍(見166頁)切小塊加入冰奶茶中即成。

1 c. starch balls (boba)*(Fig. 1)

2 tea bags (black tea)

1 ｜ 3 T. powdered creamer

⅓ c. honey or sugar

ice cubes as desired

1

1 Boil plenty of water and add the boba; cook according to instructions on the package. When done, pour the boba in a colander and rinse with cool running water. Set aside.

2 Boil 3 cups of water and steep the tea bags for several minutes; remove tea bags. Add 1 to the tea to make milk tea, stir, let cool. Add ice cubes and the boba to the milk tea. This tea can be enjoyed hot or cold.

* Starch balls, which are made of tapioca and sweet potato starch, can vary greatly depending on the brand. Some can be cooked within 10 minutes while the dry variety requires additional simmering. Following the written instructions on the package prior to cooking is essential. When cooked perfectly, boba becomes soft and chewy. Once refrigerated, the cooked boba can harden. Therefore, using them the same day they are cooked is advisable.

■ Boba Milk Tea is enormously popular among urban youth. Increasingly, it can be found in trendy Asian style cafes and tea-shops in cities in the U.S. Originated in Taiwan, the earlier versions of Boba were smaller and sometimes white, generating names such as Pearls, Black Pearls, or Tapioca Balls. As the starch balls evolved and later became larger, the playful name, Boba, increasingly replaced its original names.

The traditional Boba Milk Tea is prepared by placing brewed black tea, creamer, syrup, and ice cubes into a shaker. The mixture is shaken several times to yield bubbles in the tea, and is poured into a glass containing cooked boba and then served.

■ Boba Milk Tea can be enjoyed in great variety: with red beans, mung beans, coconut, or coffee jello. The cooked boba can be added to iced coffee, Thai milk tea, Hong Kong-style coffee milk tea (half coffee and half milk tea), or blended fruit smoothies.

MILK TEA WITH COFFEE JELLO Cut coffee jello (p.166) into small pieces and place into iced milk tea; serve.

索引

WEI-CHUAN COOKBOOKS

CHINESE CUISINE
APPETIZERS, CHINESE STYLE
CHINESE COOKING MADE EASY
CHINESE CUISINE
CHINESE COOKING FAVORITE HOME DISHES
CHINESE COOKING FOR BEGINNERS [1]
FISH, CHINESE STYLE MADE EASY [2]
SHELLFISH, CHINESE STYLE MADE EASY [2]

CHINESE REGIONAL CUISINE
CHINESE CUISINE, BEIJING STYLE
CHINESE CUISINE, CANTONESE STYLE
CHINESE CUISINE, SHANGHAI STYLE
CHINESE CUISINE, SZECHWAN STYLE
CHINESE CUISINE, TAIWANESE STYLE

GARNISHES
CHINESE GARNISHES [3]
GREAT GARNISHES

HEALTHFUL COOKING
CHINESE HERB COOKING FOR HEALTH
CHINESE HOME COOKING FOR HEALTH
LOW-CHOLESTEROL CHINESE CUISINE
SIMPLY VEGETARIAN
VEGETARIAN COOKING

INTERNATIONAL CUISINE
INDIAN CUISINE
JAPANESE CUISINE [4]
KOREAN CUISINE
MEXICAN COOKING MADE EASY [5]

ONE DISH MEALS FROM POPULAR CUISINES [2]
SINGAPOREAN, MALAYSIAN, & INDONESIAN CUISINE
THAI COOKING MADE EASY [6]
VIETNAMESE CUISINE

RICE & NOODLES
CHINESE RICE & NOODLES
NOODLES, CLASSICAL CHINESE COOKING
RICE, CHINESE HOME-COOKING
RICE, TRADITIONAL CHINESE COOKING

SPECIALTIES
CHINESE DIM SUM
CHINESE SNACKS, REVISED
CREATIVE CHINESE OVEN COOKING
INTERNATIONAL BAKING DELIGHTS

COMPACT COOKBOOK SERIES
BEEF [7]
CHICKEN [7]
SOUP! SOUP! SOUP!
TOFU! TOFU! TOFU!
VEGETABLES [7]
VERY! VERY! VEGETARIAN!

VIDEOS
CHINESE GARNISHES I [8]
CHINESE GARNISHES II [8]

OTHERS
CARVING TOOLS

• ALL COOKBOOKS ARE BILINGUAL (ENGLISH/CHINESE) UNLESS FOOTNOTED OTHERWISE •

1. Also available in English/Spanish, French/Chinese, and German/Chinese   **2.** Trilingual English/Chinese/Spanish edition
3. Bilingual English/Spanish Only   **4.** Also available in Chinese/French   **5.** Also available in English/Spanish
6. Also available in English/French   **7.** English and Chinese are in separate editions   **8.** English Only

---

味全叢書

中國菜系列
中國菜
速簡中國菜
實用中國菜 [1]
實用家庭菜
美味小菜
魚 [2]
蝦、貝、蟹 [2]

省份菜
上海菜
四川菜
北京菜
台灣菜
廣東菜

拼盤·米·麵
拼盤與盤飾
盤飾精選
米麵簡餐
米食，家常篇
米食，傳統篇
麵，精華篇

健康系列
養生藥膳
養生家常菜
均衡飲食
健康素
素食

點心·烘焙·燒烤
點心專輯
飲茶食譜
實用烘焙
創意燒烤

異國風味
南洋菜
泰國菜 [4]
越南菜
印度菜
韓國菜
日本料理 [5]
墨西哥菜 [3]
簡餐 (五國風味) [2]

小食譜
豆腐
湯
家庭素食
牛肉 [6]
雞肉 [6]
蔬菜 [6]

(如無數字標註，即為中英對照版)

1. 中英、英西、中法、中德版   **2.** 中英西對照版   **3.** 中英版及英西版   **4.** 中英版及英法版   **5.** 中英版及中法版   **6.** 中文版及英文版

OTROS LIBROS DE WEI-CHUAN
EDICIONES EN ESPAÑOL

Adornos Chinos[1]
Cocina China Para Principiantes, Edición Revisada [1]
Cocina Popular de Un Solo Platillo [2]
Comida Mexicana, Fácil de Preparar [1]
Mariscos, Estilo Chino Fácil de Preparar [2]
Pescado, Estilo Chino Fácil de Preparar [2]

---

1. Disponible en ediciones bilingües Inglés/Español
2. Edición trilingüe Inglés/Chino/Español

Los Libros de Cocina Wei-Chuan se pueden comprar en E.E.U.U., Canadá y otros 20 países a través del mundo.

PLUS DE PUBLICATIONS DE WEI-CHUAN
EDITION EN FRANÇAIS

Cuisine Chinoise Pour Débutants[1]
Cuisine Thailandaise Facilitée [2]
La Cuisine Japonaise [1]

---

1. Edition Chinoise/Française
2. Edition Anglaise/Française

Les livres de cuisine Wei-Chuan Peuvent être achetés aux Etats-Unis, Canada et ving autres pays du monde.

Wei-Chuan Cookbooks can be purchased in the U.S.A., Canada and twenty other countries worldwide
1455 Monterey Pass Road, #110, Monterey Park, CA 91754, U.S.A. ● Tel: (323)261-3880 ● Fax: (323) 261-3299
E-Mail: wc@weichuancookbook.com ● Website: weichuancookbook.com

Wei-Chuan Cooking School was founded in 1961 as a subsidiary of Wei-Chuan Food Corporation, the largest food manufacturer in Taiwan. The school soon became the largest and most respected institution of its kind along the Asia-Pacific rim. Graduates include world-class chefs, institutional teachers, professional caterers, connoisseurs of Chinese and international cuisines as well as many homemakers.

As Wei-Chuan's reputation grew, requests came from all over the world for guidance and information relative to the recipes used in the cooking classes. In an effort to meet this demand, CHINESE CUISINE was written and published in 1972. The book was very successful and became the first in a series of popular Wei-Chuan Cookbooks. Wei-Chuan Publishing was founded later that same year in Taipei then subsequently established in the U.S.A. in 1978.

Wei-Chuan, long recognized as publishing the most comprehensive Chinese cuisine cookbooks, has now expanded its recipes to include other cuisines from around the world.

Wei-Chuan's success can be attributed to its commitment to provide the best quality product possible. All recipes are complemented by full color photographs. Each recipe is written simply with easy-to-follow instructions and precisely measured ingredients. Wei-Chuan stands behind its name, reputation, and commitment to remain true to the authenticity of its recipes.